W9-CPP-625

The Young Investor

The Young Investor

Projects and Activities for Making Your Money Grow

Katherine R. Bateman

CHICAGO REVIEW PRESS

Library of Congress Cataloging-in-Publication Data

Bateman, Katherine Roberta
The young investor : projects and activities for making your money
grow / Katherine R. Bateman.
    p. cm.
Includes biographical references and index.
Summary: Suggests how to make your money grow, discussing savings,
investing, stocks, and economy.
    ISBN 1-55652-396-3
    1. Investments—Juvenile literature. 2. Saving and
investment—Juvenile literature. 3. Money—Juvenile literature. 4.
Stocks—Juvenile literature. 5. Children—Finance, Personal—Juvenile
literature. [1. Finance, Personal. 2. Money. 3. Stocks. 4. Investments.] I. Title.
    HG4521 .B4225 2001
    332.6—dc21

                                    2001042105

To contact the author, write to her in care of the publisher.

Cover design: Paul Dolan Illustration
Interior design and illustration: Sean O'Neill

© 2001 by Katherine R. Bateman
All rights reserved
First edition
Published by Chicago Review Press, Incorporated
814 North Franklin Street
Chicago, Illinois 60610
ISBN-13: 978-1-55652-396-0
ISBN-10: 1-55652-396-3
Printed in the United States of America
10 9 8

To my six grandchildren—Eleanor, Arlo, T., Cauley, Asa, and Summer

Contents

Introduction

1

All About Money

2

All About Saving

6

All About the Economy

7

All About Stock Picking

8

All About All of the Above

Conclusion

ACKNOWLEDGMENTS

The following people deserve warm thanks:

Sara Schastok, for serving as matchmaker between my book and Chicago Review Press.

The staff of Chicago Review Press, who graciously walked me through each step of publishing a first book.

My agent, Irene Tierston, for taking care of the contractual part of book writing but, more importantly, for being my dear, supportive friend for the last 40 years.

The Folak family at the Lincoln Tavern and the staff of the Corner Bakery on State and Cedar, who provided friendly, supportive places to write and glasses of iced tea the minute I walked through the door.

Cherise Chico, who bailed me out of a tough spot with her word processing skills.

Cadmus Hicks, even though the economic data he put together for me didn't make it into the book.

Billy Ray Fawns, for being so open and forthcoming about each step of his saving and investment plans. His story carries the concepts of investing into reality.

My three children, T., Lindsey, and Margret, two for providing me with such fine grandchildren and one for listening often and supportively to long passages of newly written chapters when he called from Japan.

And, finally, Richard, who has helped me build a contented, creative base from which to work.

A Letter to Parents and Grandparents

OR WHY I WROTE THIS BOOK

IN 1996, WHEN my oldest grandchild turned 10—or "moved into double digits," as she says—I made plans to give money to each of my grandchildren when they reached their teen years. I wanted to teach them a respect for money and how to invest it, but most of all I wanted them to be comfortable with money and investing concepts. I wanted them to know what people were talking about when they discussed emerging markets, rising interest rates, or consumer spending. I wanted them to be fluent in the language of business.

That summer I began to jot down notes to include in a short set of guidelines. My notes expanded over time as I realized that there was more to tell than the actual investment process. I needed to teach them about savings, but I also needed to discuss the concept of money. I wanted my grandchildren to understand some basic things about the economy, to become familiar with terms like inflation and recession and government agencies such as the Federal Reserve Board. I wanted them to know how and why major weather events affect investments. I wanted them to know how to read the stock tables in the *Wall Street Journal* or the *New York Times*.

My notes continued to grow. By this time I also had a set of cards with definitions. I've always appreciated glossaries, so I decided I would give my grandkids one, too, as well as phone numbers and Internet addresses for additional resources at their fingertips. When it was all done, I had a lengthy set of guidelines and a huge pile of scratch paper notes that totaled a book's worth of material. In the process of thinking through and collecting this material, I talked to my friends about what I was doing for my grandchildren. Their response was always the same: "When you get the book done, will you give me a copy for my kids and for me? I need to learn about it, too." That's how this book was created.

I have written it for children of that in-between—or "tween"—age. That's the tone. The data, however, is ageless. *The Young Investor* provides guidance on various types of savings plans, and it talks about compound versus simple interest. I describe Wall Street, the Dow Jones Industrial Average, and the economy. I teach young investors how to read stock and mutual fund tables.

This book also includes activities that provide hands-on experience with money and ways to make it grow. As the book continues, the concepts and activities become more complex, but readers will already have the tools to understand these from earlier chapters. My goal is to make individuals—whether they are 10, 14, or 40—conversant in saving and investing money.

This process is meant to be fun as well as educational and, potentially, financially successful. As I tell young investors in the introduction, if you save $2,000 each year between the ages of 7 and 21 and leave the money in a savings account that has an average interest rate of 7.25% until you are 65, you will have $1,000,000. That means $30,000 ($2,000 x 15 years) turns into $1,000,000 if left alone. That's the magic of compounding. If you don't start to save until age 21, you have to set aside $3,500 every year until age 65 ($154,000), with an average interest rate of 7.25% to make $1,000,000. Just imagine what your children or grandchildren can do if they have no fear of investing as teenagers and young adults.

The information in this book will be most effective if adults work with these young investors. A child can tell the adult why she or he wants to buy or sell a stock, mutual fund, or savings bond. The adult, however, must do the actual transaction. This is explained in the Introduction, and, if you've never done this before, *The Young Investor* includes scripts to guide you through these phone conversations.

I have one note to add. My grandchildren have read an early draft of the manuscript and asked friends for questions they might have if someone talked to them about investing. All of these questions are addressed in *The Young Investor*. But what truly warmed my heart was what my 11-year-old granddaughter said after reading the first draft of this book. She said, "Oh, Grandma, I just wish I had some money to invest." She didn't know that soon she would have some.

—Katherine R. Bateman
May 2001

Introduction
THE WARM-UP, INCLUDING THE GOAL

STARTING WHEN I was little—six or seven—my mother and father made me put most of my birthday and Christmas money into a piggy bank to save for a bicycle. They had me do this even though, right then, I really wanted things like a candy bar or a comic book. Now I see they had the right idea, but it was only half right. If I had put my money into a real bank instead of my piggy bank, I would have accumulated the money for my bike much sooner, because a bank would pay me to save my money. My money would make more money.

The Young Investor is all about how to make your money make money. First I'll explain about money itself—what it is and how we buy it. I want to make you comfortable with the idea of saving and investing, and this book will give you the tools to do it.

The first time that many of you bought money was when you were born. Your grandparents may have paid you to struggle into this world by giving you a gift of money at your birth. Never mind that it was your mother who did most of the struggling; you were the one who received the money in some sort of savings account.

Next I'll cover the different ways to save money. Banks are not the only place to put your savings. You can also save your money at a special kind of company called a "savings and loan," or you can buy something called a "certificate of deposit." You can shop for the best deal on your savings money just as you do for a new pair of gym shoes endorsed by your favorite basketball star.

I'll then explore the investment world. Savers can also be investors. The question is what to invest in—stocks, bonds, or mutual funds, or some of each. I'll explain each of these savings tools and what they do for you and your money. How to decide where to invest is a major focus of *The Young Investor*. I'll also explain how investment markets work.

I'll cover Wall Street next, including how it got its name and what people mean when they refer to "the market." This interesting story will give you clues about this country's history. You'll also learn about the different types of markets available for stock investments and how each works.

Once you know about investments and how the market works, I'll teach you how to learn more about particular stocks. In order to make good decisions, you'll need to learn how to read certain stock tables in newspapers. Eventually you'll be able to show your friends how to do it.

Next I'll cover the economy, and explain why floods and hurricanes affect you just as much as summers that are too hot or winters that are too cold. You may end up reading the paper, looking at the weather channel, and listening to world news. Knowing what's going on in the world may determine how much money you make on your investments, which in turn will affect how much you invest.

Next comes the reward—select a stock to (hopefully) make money. There are hundreds of companies you can invest in by buying stock in those companies. Here, I'll offer you some guidelines to help you narrow your stock choices. I'll show you how to figure out if the companies you think you might want to invest in are good choices.

The final chapter provides a lot of information about making invest-ments, including phone numbers, on-line sources, and books to read. You have to be a certain age to buy or sell stocks. If you're not that age, you'll have to tell an adult how to do it for you. When you reach 18 or 21 (depending on what state you live in) you'll be able to make these deci-sions and do these transactions yourself.

This book includes a glossary of terms for a handy reference as you go through these chapters. It will also prove a handy resource for grown-ups to help them understand what you mean when you say something like, "Since the Fed seems to have controlled inflation without putting the country into a recession, I think I'll invest in a start-up tech stock."

To help you learn how to save and invest, I'm going to give you a real life example of someone who did—Billy Ray Fawns. I met Billy Ray in Mount Sterling, Kentucky, where I have a house. He mowed my lawn for me. One day, when we talked about his mowing business, I realized Billy Ray was born with a desire to save money. I won't tell you the whole story now. I'll just say that at age 6, Billy Ray made his first money, and by age 21, he had saved enough money to buy a piece of farmland. One more thing you should know about Billy Ray is that he was a basketball star in high school and college. People in Mount Sterling still know him as "the Legend."

I have friends in their forties and fifties who are afraid to buy stock or mutual funds. They don't know how to even begin or what to say, plus they are embarrassed to ask questions for fear people will think they're dumb. I don't want that to happen to you. I want you to feel confident about saving and investing, about the economy, and about picking stocks. I don't care whether you buy stocks or mutual funds. I just don't want you to be shy when it comes to asking questions about money. As you'll see, Billy Ray asked a lot of questions, and people loved to answer him. It made them feel good.

It's a good idea to be familiar with ideas and words that have to do with money. If you are, then when you get your first job you'll already know how to save, you'll understand the power of *compounding* (you'll learn about this in Chapter 2), and you won't lose any time in saving for a car, a house, or even a fine bass or cello.

Did you know that if you save $2,000 each year between the ages of 7 and 21 and place the money in a savings account that has an average interest rate of 7.25% until you are 65, then you will have $1,000,000. If you don't start saving until age 21, you will have to save $3,500 a year every year until age 65 to have your million. Just think about that!

All About Money

WHAT IS IT, AND WHERE DOES IT COME FROM?

How to Buy Money

BEFORE YOU CAN save money, you need to have some to save. In the introduction I said you buy money. You can buy it in a number of ways. The most common way to buy money is in exchange for a skill you have. You can earn money for chores in your home such as taking out the trash, washing the family car, or cutting the grass. You can earn it by threading needles for the neighbor across the street who can't see so well anymore. You can earn it by feeding and playing with your best friend's cat while her family is out of town.

Whatever skill you have to sell, the end result is that someone pays you for your effort. The amount you are paid depends on the level of skill or the length of time required to complete the job, and sometimes it's a combination of both. This is how the adults in your family earn money—they exchange their skills for their paychecks. Then they take their paychecks and pay the babysitter and the grocer and all the other people who do things for your family.

Another common way to buy money is to exchange it for something you own, such as a sweater that you don't wear anymore, duplicate baseball cards, a key chain collection that your grandmother added to each year until you were 10, or five special Star Wars figures that you received as a gift when you were 7. The amount you are paid is based on what you and the buyer think is a fair price. If either of you think the price is not fair, the exchange won't happen.

The History of Money

You've heard people say—usually people like parents—that money doesn't grow on trees. It doesn't. It actually doesn't grow anywhere. It's printed by the United States government, or the Japanese government, or the French or Nigerian governments. Every government prints its own money, or *currency*.

The first money was not metal coins or paper as we have now. The first money was salt. In ancient China people paid for something they wanted to buy in salt. In ancient Rome soldiers were paid in salt. The word for salt in Latin—the language the Romans used—was *sal*. When your parents talk about their salaries they are using a word from the history of money, because this word comes from the Roman word *sal*.

Before there was paper or metal money, other things were used to pay for the things people needed. In some

Currency Names
Currency in different countries goes by different names. In the United States we call it the *dollar*. Here's what currency is called in some other countries.

Brazil	cruzado
France	franc
Italy	lira
Germany	mark
Spain	peso
England	pound
India	rupee
Russia	ruble
Peru	sol
Japan	yen

countries money was made from stone, as on the Yap Islands; whales' teeth were used for money in Fiji; elephant hair was the currency in Africa; and tobacco was used as money on the Solomon Islands.

About 2500 B.C., or 4,500 years ago, precious metals like gold, silver, and copper began to be used as money. Coins found from ancient Mesopotamia (now called Iraq and Iran) weren't perfect circles like our coins, but they did have pictures stamped on them as ours do today. You can find some of these coins at museums or at coin collection shops.

Search for Old Coins

Go on a search for old coins. See if you can find a coin collector in your town. Look in the Yellow Pages of the phone book under "Coins." If you can't find a listing under "Coins," look under "Numismatics." *Numismatics* means the study or collection of coins and paper money. When you find a coin collector, ask an adult to take you to his store. When you arrive, ask the store owner to show you his oldest coins. Then ask him to tell you about the coins he's showing you. If you say you're interested in numismatics, he will probably tell you a whole lot.

The Smithsonian Museum and the United States Treasury, both in Washington, D.C., have excellent coin collections, too.

You can also go to your local library or school library and look for books on coins or check the encyclopedia under "Coins" or "Numismatics." Your librarian can also help you search for pictures of coins on-line.

Paper money came much later. The earliest surviving money made from paper is from China. It was about the size of a piece of notebook paper and was issued a little before A.D. 1400. About 100 years before that, the Mongol warlord Kublai Khan used pieces of bark from mulberry trees for money.

Making Money in America

The United States Bureau of Engraving and Printing prints our paper money in two cities—Washington, D.C., and Fort Worth, Texas. Since money is worth a lot, there are many secrets regarding the making of money. One of the secrets is about the paper itself. We know that it's made from a mixture of linen and cotton. We also know that the paper has tiny colored nylon threads in it. But only a few people know the exact formula for making the paper that our money is printed on. Those people work for a company that has produced the paper for our money for more than 100 years. Another secret is how the ink used to print the money is made. It is slightly magnetic, but the formula is a carefully guarded secret.

Money is printed on large sheets of paper, so that a lot of dollar bills can be printed on each sheet. After 100 sheets are printed, the money is cut into single bills. The stacks of bills are bundled together until they are the size of a brick. These money bricks are then sent to banks, where people usually go to find crisp new money.

Paper money in the United States comes in different amounts, called *denominations*. These are: $1, $5, $10, $20, $50, and $100. The Bureau of Engraving prints $500 and $1,000 bills, but these big denominations are primarily for banks. Individuals can order $500 and $1,000 bills for special occasions like a big birthday or retirement party, but you can't just walk into a bank and trade five $100 bills for one $500 bill.

Our metal coins are made by the United States Bureau of the Mint in plants in Denver, San Francisco, and Philadelphia. The process of making coins is called minting. Each coin has a letter on it for the city where it was minted: *D* for Denver, *S* for San Francisco, and *P* for Philadelphia. See if you can find the letter indicating which mint made a coin in your pocket.

When metal was first used for money, the coins were made of precious metals like gold, silver, or copper. Now our coins are made from copper and nickel mixed together, because there's more copper and nickel available than gold and silver. When someone talks about the gold standard or the pound sterling, he or she is referring to a time when money was made from gold and silver.

The Money Circle

Once money is printed, it's put into circulation. Circulation is a good word for it because money circles around and around, going from one person's hands into another person's, over and over again. Sometimes this happens slowly and sometimes very quickly. Around Christmas, Chanukah, or Kwanzaa, it can circle like a whirlwind!

Here's an example of how money circles. Your sister baby-sits for the little girl on the next block. She takes the money that she's paid and buys a necklace for her best friend. The store where she buys the necklace pays the clerk who sold your sister the necklace. The clerk takes his money and buys a white puppy with a black spot over its left eye for his baby sister. The dog breeder takes the money the clerk gave him in exchange for the puppy and buys a calico kitten for his wife who doesn't like dogs at all.

With all that circulation, paper money gets old and ratty and coins get so worn out that you can't read the mint mark. Dollar bills last the shortest period of time—about 15 months—because they get circulated the most. A $5, $10, or $20 bill lasts longer since these don't change hands as often.

When money gets worn out, it must be replaced. So, when a really old bill or a really beat-up coin comes into a bank, the bank teller sets it aside to exchange for new money. Armored trucks take the old money from the banks to the United States Treasury Department. These bills are shredded into tiny strips, then the strips are burned until they are just a big pile of ashes. The coins are sent to one of the three mints, dumped into a big pot, and melted. The melted metal is then minted into new coins.

> What happens if a bill gets so old it falls apart? If you have at least 51% of it or just over half, it still counts as money and can be spent. But if you have only 49% of the bill, then you're out of luck. What you have is just a yucky torn piece of scrap paper.

$ Make a Money Circle

Be a money detective and track a money circle. Starting with your allowance or the money you're paid for chores, write down where your money came from and where your money went. Go as far back as you can and as far forward as you can. See how close it comes to making a circle. Refer to the example given on page 5 if you get stuck.

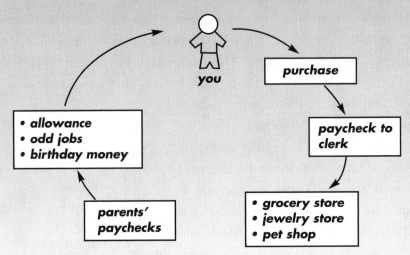

Invite your friends to do it, too. See how much of a circle all of you can make. Most times the ends won't meet, but they'll always go part way around.

Not All Money Is Printed with Secret Ink

Did you know that no cash actually changes hands for the majority of purchases in this country? About 50 years ago almost everything bought and sold was paid for with cash. Now we use other forms of money. It's not mulberry bark or salt; it's paper made from trees, or it's plastic. Checks are a common way to pay for things. This is the paper that replaces money. Credit cards are made of plastic, and people often use one of these to pay for something instead of cash.

Many people keep money in banks. In order to keep track of every-one's money, the bank gives each person a number that applies only to that person's money. Your number is your *account number*. It's sort of like having a locker number at school. All your stuff is safe from friends who want to borrow things without asking when it's locked in your own locker. There are many kinds of bank accounts. Right now, though, I'll talk just about *checking accounts*.

Here's how checking accounts work. You have some birthday money and some cash from chores you did for a family member, friend, or neighbor. You take this money to a bank. You tell one of the people sitting behind a desk that you want to open a checking account. She gives you a form to fill out that asks for your name, address, age, and social security number. You may even be asked for your mother's maiden name, her last name at birth. This is for security purposes, in case your checkbook is ever lost or stolen. Then you have to sign a form so the bank will be able to keep a record of exactly how you sign your name. If you are under 18 years old, the bank will make someone over age 18 sign his or her name, too. It's the law.

So, you've filled out the form and signed it, and you've given the bank the money you've earned. The bank then gives you a checkbook that contains 25 checks and a check register, where you record all the checks you write to keep track of your money. A checkbook is small enough to carry around with you. When you carry your checks, you don't have to carry money. Many people like paying for things with checks exactly for this reason. If you lose your checkbook it can be replaced. If you lose your cash, it's gone for good.

One cold winter afternoon you decide that you absolutely have to buy a new two-CD boxed set that you saw advertised. So, instead of taking cash, you grab your checkbook and head to the nearest music store. At the checkout counter you see a notice that says the store will accept checks if you have a picture ID. Since you have your school ID, you write out a check for $43.50. All you have to do is write in the date and the name of the music store where it says "Pay to the order of." Then you write in the amount of the purchase—in this case, $43.50—in the box and then write out the amount in words on the line below that. This can stump you sometimes. I sometimes forget how to spell "forty." Next comes the easy part—signing your name—and then it's done. Hand it to the clerk and collect your CDs.

Even though your check is as good as cash, the music store is not paid in cash by the bank. In fact, no cash actually changes hands. Instead, the bank takes money out of your account and puts it into the music store's account. In other words, the bank transfers funds from one account to another, and it does it all electronically. But there's a catch: the bank will only transfer funds if you have some funds to transfer. Your balance, or the total amount of money you have in your account, must be larger than your check amount. The check register in your checkbook is designed to help you keep track of your money.

Your check register is where you record an entry every time you write a check. Your register will look like the one below. Each time you write a check, you fill in the number from the top right-hand corner of the check, the date the check was written, the name of the store or person you wrote the check to, and the amount. Then you subtract this amount from your balance. That way you can keep track of just how much money you have in your account at all times.

The bank will also help you keep track of the checks you've written. Once a month the bank sends you something called a *statement*. A statement lists every check you've written over the past month, all deposits you've made, and any fees they've charged you.

NUMBER	DATE	DESCRIPTION OF TRANSACTION	PAYMENT/DEBIT (−)	√ T	FEE (IF ANY) (−)	DEPOSIT/CREDIT (+)	BALANCE
		RECORD ALL CHARGES OR CREDITS THAT AFFECT YOUR ACCOUNT					1000 00
116	3/11	Sports Plus	61 50				938 50
117	3/20	Barbara's Books	36 17				902 33
	3/15	deposit - b'day check				50 00	952 33
118	4/2	School Colors	89 00				863 33

REMEMBER TO RECORD AUTOMATIC PAYMENTS/DEPOSITS ON DATE AUTHORIZED

A deposit is the banking term to describe money that you've added to your account.

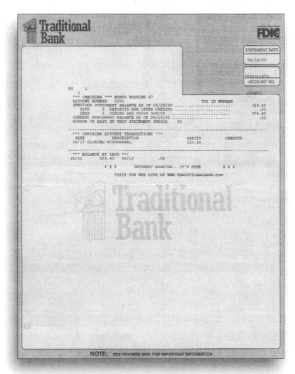

The bank statement includes directions on the back that explain exactly how to know what your balance is at the current moment. That's in case you've written a check or made a deposit since the bank mailed your statement. Balancing your checkbook is when you double check the statement's record of all checks, deposits, and fees charged to your account. You should end up with the same amount of money in your account that the statement says you have, minus any unrecorded deposits or plus any checks that have not yet cleared or been deducted from your account.

ACCOUNT BALANCING SECTION

_____ 1. Enter Ending Checking Balance from the front of this statement.

_____ 2. Enter deposits (credits) not shown on this statement.

_____ 3. Sub-Total (add line 1 and line 2).

_____ 4. Enter total of checks (debits), fees (if any), and automatic payments entered in your register, but not shown on this or previous statements.*

_____ 5. Balance (line 3 minus line 4). This amount should agree with your register.

LIST OF OUTSTANDING CHECKS & WITHDRAWALS

CHECK #	CHECK AMOUNT	CHECK#	CHECK AMOUNT
		*TOTAL (LINE 4)	

Practice Writing Checks

Practice filling out checks with these pretend checks. Write a check to Mascot Jackets for $93.27. Be sure to fill in every line on the check with the required information. Record your check in the register on the following page. Now write a check to Lofty Top Shoes for $41.33 and fill in the register. Pretend you had a balance of $393.17 in your account when you began. Be sure to subtract each check from the balance in the register and enter in the new balance. How much money do you end up with after writing these two checks?

525

73-151/421

DATE _____

Pay to
the order of _____ $ _____

_____ DOLLARS 🔒 Security features included. Details on back.

Traditional Bank
MOUNT STERLING, KENTUCKY 40353

FOR _____ MP

⑆04210151⑆ 00311375⑈ 0525

525

73-151/421

DATE _____

Pay to
the order of _____ $ _____

_____ DOLLARS 🔒 Security features included. Details on back.

Traditional Bank
MOUNT STERLING, KENTUCKY 40353

FOR _____ MP

⑆04210151⑆ 00311375⑈ 0525

		RECORD ALL CHARGES OR CREDITS THAT AFFECT YOUR ACCOUNT					
NUMBER	DATE	DESCRIPTION OF TRANSACTION	PAYMENT/ DEBIT (-)	✓ T	FEE (IF ANY) (-)	DEPOSIT/ CREDIT (+)	BALANCE $
		REMEMBER TO RECORD AUTOMATIC PAYMENTS/DEPOSITS ON DATE AUTHORIZED					

ATM Cards

When you open a checking account, most banks offer you an ATM card. ATM stands for *automated teller machine*. It's called that because you can stick your plastic card in a machine and tell the bank to do certain things to your account. The machine will do it automatically. No human is involved. An ATM lets you do your banking at any hour. At an ATM you can deposit money into or take cash out of your checking or savings account. ATMs are located almost everywhere: malls or grocery stores, on the sides of buildings, even in bank lobbies. The machine just spits out crisp tens or twenties, plus a receipt at the end to tell you how much you have left in your account. ATM machines are convenient, and most people use them as a quick way to get cash from their accounts.

ATM cards are a little safer than cash. If you lose cash, it's just gone. If you lose your ATM card, no one else can use it because you have to have a special number to use it. It's like a secret code and is called a *personal identification number* or PIN. You even get to choose your PIN so it's easy to remember.

Credit and Debit Cards

Now let's look at plastic money called credit cards and debit cards. Credit cards work like this: when you buy something and pay with a credit card, you promise the store that you will pay for your purchase at the end of the month. Actually, you are promising the store that a bank will pay for it at the end of the month. When you buy something with a credit card, a bank will pay for your purchases even if you don't have any cash in your pocket.

But there's a hitch: many banks make you pay a fee each year for the use of their credit cards, and a *bigger* hitch is that if you don't pay off your credit card bill in full each month, the bank charges you an extra fee for using their money. These fees can add up and up the longer you don't pay your balance. It's like paying more for items that, maybe, you bought on sale in the first place. And because credit cards sometimes give you a *line of credit* (total amount you can charge) far higher than you can afford to pay off easily, you can get into financial trouble. So even though credit cards have benefits, like not having to carry a lot of cash around, they have some dangers too. In the late 20th century, almost 75% of American families had at least one credit card.

Not quite as many families have debit cards, but many do. When you buy something with a debit card, the amount of your purchase is immediately subtracted from the money you have in your bank account. Instead of writing a check, you simply hand the cashier your debit card and the amount of the purchase will be automatically subtracted from your account. All you have to do is sign your name and enter the amount of the purchase in your check register.

When you use a debit card you don't have to worry about paying late fees unless you buy things that cost more money than you have in the bank. When you spend more money than you have in your account (either by writing checks or using your debit card) it's called being *over-drawn*, and it means you've tried to spend more money than you have available in your account. When you are overdrawn the bank gets very upset, and when banks get upset they make you pay a special fee. The fee may be bigger than the check you wrote that put you over your limit in the first place! People who keep track of the amount of money they have in the bank usually don't have problems with overdrawing. Since you already know how to use your check register to enter all the checks you write, the purchases you make with a debit card, your cash with-drawals or deposits at an ATM, and the deposits you make at a teller, you won't ever make the mistake of overdrawing on your account.

Billy Ray Buys Some Money

Billy Ray Fawns bought money by exchanging it for something he owned and by exchanging it for a skill. Billy Ray was born in 1977 and grew up in Mount Sterling, a town in central Kentucky with a population of about 5,200 people. Billy Ray's father is a bricklayer who owns his own business. Billy Ray says, "he worked hard for the money to support our family."

Billy Ray started making money in kindergarten and first grade by selling the fruit his mother packed in his lunch. He sold his banana or apple for a dollar. (Can you believe it?) He doesn't know how he got the idea to sell his fruit in the first place. This went on until he asked his mother if she would put two pieces of fruit in his lunch box. When she guessed what was going on, she put a stop to the fruit-for-money exchange. This didn't keep Billy Ray from selling his old tennis shoes to a classmate for $15.

Billy Ray also worked for money. When he was 11 he fell in love with a motorcycle that cost $2,000. His father told him that if he worked all summer helping with bricklaying jobs, he would match the money that Billy Ray saved. So Billy Ray worked and he saved. He worked all summer carrying bricks and mixing mortar and doing almost anything the bricklayers needed. In the evenings he mowed yards and did other odd jobs for people. At the end of the summer he had saved half the price of the motorcycle. His dad kept his promise and Billy Ray bought his cycle. But he realized something that summer—working that hard for his money taught him to respect it. And he realized something else—he wanted to figure out other ways to make money.

In this chapter you learned:
- how to buy money
- how money is made
- how money circulates
- how to write checks and use ATM and debit cards
- how to keep track of the money you have in the bank

If you only remember one thing about money, though, it should be this: Money changes hands over and over and at some point you may decide to try to stop the circulation of your money long enough to save some. But even when you think you're taking money out of circulation by saving it, you can still get paid for doing this. That's where our investment story really begins.

All About Saving

HOW TIME AND A LITTLE MATH CAN MAKE YOU RICH

Savings Accounts

THERE ARE A number of ways to save money—you can hide it in your room, bury it in the garden, have a friend keep it for you so you won't spend it in a moment of weakness—but none of these ways is very safe. You may forget where you hid your money, your dog may dig up and tear up your money if you bury it in your yard, and your friend might forget that it is your money and spend it on herself. The best place to save money is in a bank. That's what banks do—they keep money for people. At least, that's part of what they do.

15

A bank is a place that stores money for you and lets you have it back when you want it. They protect it, too, from your forgetting where you hid it, or your dog digging it up, or even losing it in a fire or flood. But, instead of paying the bank to guard your money, the bank pays you for keeping it in a *savings account*. A savings account is like a checking account, except you can't write checks. Banks pay you because they let other people borrow money from you. What you get from the bank, in exchange for letting your money be used and loaned to others, is more money. Your money is also protected by a very strong insurance policy.

This is how it works. You ask the bank to keep your money in a savings account. Just as with a checking account, you have an account number that identifies your money. Your friend George also has a savings account in the same bank. George's parents and your parents and the guy who rents you in-line skates also put money in separate savings accounts in your bank. Now the bank has a lot of money that it's keeping for everyone, separated by the different account numbers that belong to each of these people.

The winter after you opened your savings account, your sixth grade math teacher Ms. Henderson decides she wants to buy a summer home on a golf course. So she walks into your bank and asks to borrow some money to pay for the house. The bank says, "Sure you can borrow money. We've got a lot of it. But you have to pay us to let you use the money." Ms. Henderson pays the bank to borrow the money, and the bank pays you part of the money Ms. Henderson pays them. After all, your money is part of the money she borrowed. The money they pay you is called *interest*, and the interest adds up and up and up. This is how you save.

Banks are not the only places that like to guard your money and then pay you interest for this right. Savings and loan companies, usually just called savings and loans, are another great place to save your money. Savings and loans work just like banks with one big exception. They don't have to follow the same strict rules that all banks in the United States are required to follow.

The difference between banks and savings and loans is a lot like the difference between public and private schools. You have rules in your public school. They are the same rules that you and your biggest football rival and all the other public schools in your state must follow. A public school is like a bank. A private school follows its own rules. In fact, the school might have been originally established when its founders decided they didn't like the public school rules and wanted to make their own. If you have friends who go to private schools then you know they have different hall and classroom rules. Savings and loans are like private schools. They are owned by a group of people who are called *investors*, and they make their own rules.

There's a very important rule that savings and loan companies have that is different from banks: the savings and loan board members—sort of like school principals—decide how much they pay members (like you) to take care of and to lend your money. Banks pay interest based on numbers the government thinks are best. Savings and loans set their own interest levels. They can pay as much as they want, so sometimes you get more interest if you open a savings account with a savings and loan company than with a bank.

Money Market Accounts and Certificates of Deposit

There's another easy way to save money. You can put your money in a *money market account*. A money market account is a savings account with a boost. You buy money market accounts through banks or investment companies. Money market accounts give you a little more interest than a straight savings account, because the money in the accounts is invested for you by people who are trained to make investments. The investments are safe ones, so you don't have to be afraid of losing any money, plus you can write checks against the money in your account. There are certain rules, like checks you write have to be at least $500, or some other pretty big amount. You also have to pay the bank that holds your account a small portion of the money it makes for you for this service. Even after subtracting this fee you usually still earn more money than in a savings account.

There's one more place to save money. You can buy *certificates of deposit*, or CDs, from banks. (Not all CDs play music.) CDs are for savers who won't need a certain amount of their savings for the next six months or year or two years. When you buy a CD, the bank pays you a little more interest than it pays for savings accounts or money market accounts. The longer the period of time of the CD, the greater the interest you get paid. If you decide you won't need $500 for the next two years, and you buy a two-year CD, you will earn more interest than if you buy a six-month CD. There's a hitch though: if you take your money out before the term of the CD is up, the bank will charge you a penalty, so you will lose money instead of making it. There's a good reason you make more money with CDs. It's worth money to the bank when you promise that it can use your money for a known and longer length of time. This is why a bank will pay you more interest on a two-year CD than on a six-month CD. This is also why the bank charges you a penalty fee if you cancel your CD early, because your money has already been lent to other people to buy houses, cars, or boats.

Remember, you can shop for the best interest rate just as your folks shop for the best price on a new car or van. Here's how it stacks up. You are paid a certain amount of interest on a savings account. For banks that amount is pretty much determined by the government. (I'll explain how this amount is determined in Chapter 6.) You earn a little more interest if you put your money in a money market account. You earn a little more interest still if you purchase a CD, especially if it is a one- or two-year CD.

The Power of Compounding

Knowing different places to put your savings is just half of making money. The other half—and in some ways the most important half—is understanding about time and the power of compounding.

You can earn interest in one of two ways. One is called *simple interest* and it is, in fact, simple to describe. Simple interest means that you will get a certain amount of interest for a determined amount of time. For example, you may be told that if you open a savings account with $100 and keep it in the bank for one year, you will earn 6% interest. That means you will earn $6 at the end of the year ($100 x 0.06 = $6). That would give you savings of $106 for the year ($100 + $6 = $106). That's simple interest.

The other kind of interest is called *compound interest.* Compound interest has a lot to do with time. Here is where a little math comes in. Remember when I said at the beginning of this book that if you saved $2,000 a year between ages 7 and 21 and left it in the bank earning an average of 7.25% a year, you would have $1 million at age 65 without ever saving again? Well, that's the power of compounding. When interest is compounded, banks or savings and loans pay you interest on the interest you've earned for each day or month you have money in your savings account. Here's how it works: You open a savings account with $100 in a bank that pays 6% compound interest. The bank will say it is paying 6% Annual Percentage Rate, or APR. You divide this rate over 12 months to get the monthly interest rate. In this example that's 6%, or 0.06, divided by 12 months equals 0.005 interest a month, and 0.005 x $100 = $100.50. So, at the end of the first month you have $100.50. The next month the bank pays you interest not just for the $100 you originally put in, but also for the money (50 cents) it paid you to keep it there. At the end of the second month you have $101.00, and so on until at the end of the year you have $106.17.

That's the power of compounding. It's like magic, except there are no tricks. You just sit there and watch it happen month after month after month and year after year. If your $100 had earned simple interest at the same 6%, you would have made $6 over the year. You may think that 17 cents is not much difference, but just imagine if you had $500 in your savings account, or $1,000. The difference between simple and compound interest increases as you put more money into your account. Your original $100 will keep compounding, and by the end of 5 years you'll have $134 (instead of $130 from a simple savings account) and at the end of 10 years you'll have $179 in your account (instead of $160).

$100 at 6% Interest Compounded Monthly			
Month 1	100.50	Month 7	103.55
Month 2	101.00	Month 8	104.07
Month 3	101.51	Month 9	104.59
Month 4	102.02	Month 10	105.11
Month 5	102.53	Month 11	105.64
Month 6	103.04	Month 12	106.17

Compare Interest Rates at Banks and Savings and Loans

Search for different banks and savings and loan companies. You can walk or ride your bike or watch while you're riding in a car. You can also look up the names of different banks or savings and loans in the *Yellow Pages* under "Banks" or under "Savings and Loan Companies." Write down these names and phone numbers. Select three. Call or stop by each one to find out what interest rates they offer on their savings accounts. Sometimes you can tell the bank's rate by a sign in the window that reads something like "5.25% APR." Ask if the interest rate is simple or compound.

Copy the table below to record the information you gather.

Name of Bank or Savings and Loan	Phone Number	Account Type: Savings (S) Money Market (MM)	Simple (S) or Compound (C) Interest

Date of First Call	Interest Rate at First Call	Date of Second Call	Interest Rate at Second Call

One month later, contact these places again and ask the interest rate. Fill in the date and the new interest rate. Is it the same or has it changed? If it has changed, try to figure out why. The chapter on the economy (Chapter 6) will help you do this. You can also ask an adult or the bank itself to explain the change. Which place offered the highest return last month? Which one this month? Is it the same?

Saving money is the first step to investing. In the beginning, it seems hard to do—even impossible when you think of the CD (that's compact disc) you could buy this week, or that great bracelet like the one your best friend bought on sale. But once you start saving, it's hard to stop, because you see your savings grow as the bank or savings and loan pays you interest every single month. You begin to feel the magic and dream of how much more money you'll have the longer you wait to spend it. You may even become so enthusiastic that you'll add even more of your allowance, chore, or babysitting money into your account.

Calculate Your Interest Earnings

This activity will show you how to figure out how much money you'll have in a savings account in one year if you have money to invest.

Go back to the list of interest rates you collected from banks and savings and loans in the previous activity. Pick an amount of money that you would like to save. Take the dollar amount you've chosen and the interest rate the first bank will pay you. Use the math and example below to help figure out how much you would have from each of your three banks or savings and loans in one year. Remember that even small amounts of interest add up over time—that's the power of compounding.

Calculate Your Interest Earnings

Annual Interest Rate/12 = Monthly Interest Rate
Savings Amount x Monthly Interest Rate + 1 =
Savings Plus Interest Earned for One Month

Here's an example. You have $200 to open an account. Bank A is offering an annual interest rate of 5% on its savings accounts. It requires a minimum initial deposit of $200. This is how you calculate your interest earnings:

1. Change 5% into a decimal number (0.05).

2. Divide .05 by 12 to get the monthly interest rate (0.00416).

3. Calculate your savings at the end of month 1 by adding 1 to the monthly interest rate and multiplying by your savings amount ($200.00). Your result should be $200.83. Repeat this step using the new savings total for each month.

4. Calculate a couple more years until you understand this calculation. Copy the table below to organize your information. Now calculate your interest earnings using the bank rates you collected in the previous activity. Create tables like the one here to organize your information and make it easier to compare banks and their rates.

$200	5% Interest Rate
Month 1	$200.83
Month 2	$201.63
Month 3	$202.44
Month 4	

Bank Name:	Bank A
Annual Interest Rate:	5%
Amount Needed to Open a New Savings Account:	$200

Billy Ray Starts to Save

Billy Ray felt the magic of saving. When he was eight his parents started a savings account for him with a gift of $500. From that time on, whenever he received birthday or Christmas money, he deposited it into his savings account. He didn't buy many toys, as his friends did when they were given some money. He was having more fun wandering around outside and practicing basketball. So he just tucked his money away.

One day he realized that the more money he had in his savings account, the more quickly it seemed to grow. He didn't know anything about the power of compounding at that point, even though in school he had done those math problems where Mary has $100 and she puts it in a bank and earns 5% interest. Somehow he never thought about those problems as real life. They were just homework.

Billy Ray woke up to this reality when he began watching his savings account grow—faster and faster—and it made him want to save more. Whenever he cut grass or shoveled snow, he put half of the money in his savings account and kept half for his own spending money. He called it "paying himself." As he watched the money accumulate in his savings account, he began to try to figure out how to make his money grow even faster.

One day, just like Billy Ray, you will look at your total savings and be shocked by how much you have. That might also be the moment you think to yourself, "I wonder if there's a way to make even more interest than I'm getting now." There is. That's when you become an investor.

In this chapter you learned:
- about savings, money market accounts, and CDs that don't play music
- how to calculate compound interest
- the secret of time and how it earns money

What you don't know yet is how personalities fit into the investing picture. You'll learn about this in the next chapter.

All About Investing

HOW TO MAKE MONEY MAKE MORE MONEY

Risk Tolerance

NOW IT'S TIME to get down to the heart of the matter—making money. You have a little money saved and you like the feeling of watching it grow, but you'd like to make it grow faster. Are there ways to make more interest on your money than by keeping it in a bank or savings and loan? Yes! This chapter is all about how you can make your money make more money; that is, how to invest your money. You will learn how to spend some of your savings to make a little more money on something called an investment. If you follow one of these strategies for making money that I'll detail here, then you will be an investor.

Investing is not just about spending and making money. It's about time and personality types. When people talk about investing they use words like *compounding* (remember, that has to do with time) and they talk about *risk tolerance* (that has to do with personality type). Both of these factors are important. Compounding was covered in the last chapter. Risk tolerance has to do with how people approach life. You know from watching family members or friends that some people are afraid to try new things. They are afraid to jump into something like playing lacrosse or taking dance lessons or going to the mall by themselves. On the other hand, there are some people who don't seem to be scared of anything. These are the people who are the first to answer a want ad for a job even though they've never worked for anyone in their lives, or they will raise their hands in class even if they're not sure they really know the answers. Some people are a combination of both extremes. In fact, most people are combinations, but they tend to be more one way than the other no matter what they do. That has to do with their personalities. Neither way is good or bad. It's just one of the ways that people differ.

The way people tend to act and the things they tend to worry about show their risk tolerance for investments along with everything else. Some people are afraid to lose their savings, so they will be very careful when they invest. They have a low risk tolerance. Other people are willing to take a chance to make a lot of money, even if it means they might lose some of their savings. They have a high risk tolerance. You are the only one who knows what you will feel comfortable doing. You might even have to try a riskier investment or two before you know for sure. But whether you have a low or a high risk tolerance, there are investments available for you.

Make a Risk Tolerance Chart

Make a list of 10 of your friends or family members. Think about the things they do and the way they behave. Observe the behavior of each person on your list for a while. Note if they like adventures, try new things, or speak up in class often. Do they dislike being called on in class even when they have their homework done and know the answer? Are they afraid of trying new things?

Make a chart like the one pictured here. This will help you keep track of the level of risk tolerance for your 10 friends and family members. Divide your chart into 12 rows and 4 columns. Write your friends' and family members' names in the far left column. On top of the next column write "Does Not Take Chances." Write "Sometimes Takes Chances" on top of the third column and "Will Take Chances" on top of the last column. Place an *X* in the box that you think best describes each person after you've had some time to observe them. In the last row, write in your name and place an *X* in the box that best describes your behavior. Ask your friends where they'd place you on this risk tolerance scale. Did they tell you exactly what you marked down for yourself? Get their feedback on how you charted the other people on the list. Do you agree or disagree?

Name	Does Not Take Chances	Sometimes Takes Chances	Will Take Chances

Bonds

United States Savings Bonds

Now that you know about risk tolerance, it's time to think about what investments to make. The two most common investments are stocks and bonds. Bonds are investments that have less risk, and therefore are good investment choices for people with low risk tolerances. Bonds are a good, steady investment. They earn money for you on a regular basis, with hardly any risk that you will lose your money. That's why bonds feel comfortable to investors with a low risk tolerance. Bonds help you make more money than bank, savings and loan, or money market accounts pay you.

What exactly is a bond? A *bond* is an agreement between you and another party, stating that it can use—or borrow—your money for a set period of time. It can be three months, six months, a year, 2 years, 5 years, or even 25 years. In return for letting this other party use your money it will pay you, just as a bank pays you, but it will pay you more than the bank does.

Just as banks will pay you to save money, the federal government will, too. The federal government is the United States government (different from state government) or, as some older people say, "Uncle Sam." (Uncle Sam is big with grandparents.)

Grandparents, aunts, uncles, and friends of the family like to buy U.S. savings bonds to give as gifts on a birthday or holiday. But anyone can buy savings bonds—even you.

The most popular savings bond is called the Series EE bond. You can purchase this type of bond for as little as $50 or as much as $15,000.

Savings bonds are pretty neat because what you are really doing is letting Uncle Sam—that's the United States of America—borrow money from you! Here's how it works. The U.S. government sells savings bonds. When you buy one, you are saying to the government, "You may use my money for a certain number of years." It can be as few as 5 years or as many as 30 years. You give the government some of your money, say $50, and in a few years (based on the current interest rate) the government gives you back $100. The difference between the $50 and the $100 is your interest, just like from a bank or savings and loan company. But this time, you have the government's IOU. It's a fancy piece of paper that looks kind of like money—that's the bond.

At the end of the time you and the government agreed on for the loan, the bond "reaches maturity," which means the time period of the bond has expired and you can now collect the face value of the bond. (Since you paid much less than this, the difference is your profit! When the bonds reach maturity, you can take them to any bank. The bank gives back the amount of money you lent Uncle Sam, plus what he agreed to pay you for the loan. What you get back is your investment return.

Investment return is another way of saying interest earned. You can find out the current interest rate on U.S. Savings Bonds by calling (800) 487-2663.

There are many kinds of bonds besides savings bonds, but there are only three that you need to know about right now. They are called treasury bonds, municipal bonds, and corporate bonds. You may not want to buy any of them yet, but you need to know about them for when you get your first real job or if you make a lot of money on your investments before then.

Search for a Savings Bond

Go on a savings bond search. Ask a parent if you or anyone else in your family has ever received a savings bond. Ask if you can see it. It might be locked in a safe deposit box for safekeeping.

Next go to a bank and ask someone who works there to explain to you how to buy a savings bond. It's best to ask one of the bank workers who sits behind a desk, because they have more time to help customers.

Treasury Bonds

Treasury bonds—or "treasuries," as they are usually called—are IOUs from the federal government (Uncle Sam again). Treasuries are really just bigger savings bonds. Sometimes the government runs out of money just when it needs to pay for something, and just as you might ask your best friend if you can borrow a little money until your next allowance, Uncle Sam asks you if he can borrow from you.

When you buy treasury bonds, you are lending money to the government. To prove that you lent it money, the government gives you an IOU. The IOU is a contract with a promise to pay you back at the time you agreed on. The key is that you are paid back with interest. Sometimes the interest is paid back at the end of the contract and sometimes it is paid along the way.

There's a different name for each length of time you lend the government money. These are:

- treasury *bill*: less than a year
- treasury *note*: 1 to 10 years
- treasury *bond*: more than 10 years

You should buy treasury bonds through a mutual fund group when you first start to buy them. (Mutual fund groups are covered later in this chapter.) You can buy them in smaller denominations if you buy them this way. *Denomination* is just another word for amount. Although you can buy treasuries for as little as $1,000, the standard denominations are $10,000 for individual investors and $100,000 for banks and brokerage firms.

Municipal Bonds

Another kind of bond is a municipal bond. They're interesting because so many of the things you see and use every day may exist because of municipal bonds, such as your school, a hospital, a bridge, or even a nearby jail. The water that comes out of your faucet may get to your home because of a municipal water bond. This might also be true for your electricity—it might come from an electric power bond.

Cities or towns, and even counties and states, are officially referred to as *municipalities*. That's why bonds that help pay for schools or hospitals are called *municipal* bonds. When a town or a city wants to build a new school or parking garage or hospital, they often ask the people who live there (and even people who don't) to lend it some money to finance or pay for the project.

The people who agree to lend money to the city—or municipality—get an IOU. They invest in the city's project. The city then agrees to pay the investors money—usually every six months—for letting it use the money. The amount of interest paid is based on the length of the loan. Investors who agree to lend their money for five years are paid a higher interest amount than those who will lend the city money for only one year. If you agree to let the municipality use your money for 30 years, the interest is even higher.

At the end of the contract, the municipality gives back the full amount of the loan. The original amount that you let the municipality borrow is called the *principal*. (This is not the top dog at your school, even if it's spelled the same way.) But don't forget that even before you get your principal back, you have been paid every six months to let the municipality borrow your money.

The thing that's especially nice about municipal bonds is that you can look at structures in your own hometown and know you helped build them. Another really nice thing about them is that you usually don't have to pay taxes on the money you earn while your money is on loan. That's not as important to you right now as it is to your parents. (I'll talk more about taxes in the last chapter.) One last thing, since municipal bonds sell in pretty big denominations, it's best to buy them through a mutual fund. This way you can invest as little as $500 or $1,000 in a group of municipal bonds. Otherwise you would have to buy one bond for $5,000—the usual denomination size.

Corporate Bonds

Finally, you should know about corporate bonds. Corporate bonds are similar to treasury and municipal bonds. The only difference is the borrower. Rather than lending money to the government or a municipality, people who invest in corporate bonds lend money to a private company for a private purpose. Corporate bonds are fun because you can lend money to companies that you know about, such as McDonald's, Wendy's, Chuck E. Cheese, Nike, or The Gap.

When you invest in corporate bonds, you let companies use your money to expand. Sometimes this might be to build a new cafeteria for employees or a second parking lot; other times it may be to update the company's computer equipment and wiring. Your money may even make it possible for the company to build a whole new plant. The company believes that the improvement it wants to make will increase its profitability, and it will be able to pay you back with interest out of its increased profits.

Corporate bonds pay a little more interest than treasuries or municipal bonds. That's because there is a little more risk involved. Companies are businesses and they exist because people buy what they sell. So, if you and your friends and many other people stop buying this company's products, then the company may go out of business. Needless to say, when a company goes out of business, it is not making the money it needs to pay back investors.

Bond Market Risk Rankings

When you invest in the bond market—that's lingo for when you buy bonds—you have a low level of overall risk. But there are different degrees of low-level risk among these various bond products. The risk ranks like this, from the lowest to the highest: government bonds—that's savings bonds and treasuries; then municipal bonds—that's bonds of cities, counties, and states; and then corporate bonds—that's bonds of private companies like Kellogg or Pepsi. Still, even when you invest in corporate bonds, you do not have the risk levels that you have for stocks, as you'll see in a minute.

$ Discover What's Built by Bonds

Walk or ride your bike around your neighborhood or town and look for schools and hospitals. Ask your principal if the school was built with municipal bonds. You might have to explain what a municipal bond is, but you can do that.

If you can get to a hospital, ask the receptionist or person at the information desk to direct you to the person who can tell you if the hospital was built with municipal bonds. Again, you may have to explain what a municipal bond is. You may also have to explain why you want to know. Just say it's for an investment project you're working on. Keep asking until you find the right person. You will probably have some interesting conversations with these people, especially if you end up talking to the director of the hospital. It will be an adventure and one that you'll talk about with pride.

Stocks

It's time to move on to stock. What is stock anyway? *Stock* is the amount of money a business company is worth. There's a special term for the money in a business. It's called *capital*. So, another way to define stock is to say that stock is the capital of a business company. Some companies, like automobile manufacturers, have a huge amount of capital. Other companies have a smaller amount of capital, such as start-up technology firms.

Imagine a company as a huge pie. The pie is the company's stock. Now picture the pie cut into 100 pieces. Each piece of the pie is a share of the stock. Sometimes a company decides to sell some of its stock. It lets the public—that's us—buy pieces, or shares, of the pie. In fact, when a private company sells its stock, it's called "going public." When you buy a share of stock, you become part owner of the company, and you become a shareholder.

A company that goes public usually wants to keep the biggest part of the pie for itself. That's in case some of the shareholders don't agree with the way the company is being run. There can be big arguments at shareholders' meetings, where people yell and scream at the people who manage the company. But the shareholders with the most shares get the most votes, so if the company that sold the stock in the first place owns the most shares, it can do what it feels is in its best interests.

A company may decide to sell different kinds of stock shares to the public. They can sell *common* or *preferred* shares. There might be A and B shares. There might even be G and H shares. Each type is slightly different than the other, but those differences are not so important to you now. All you need to know is that they exist. The most common type of stock to buy is the common share. Makes sense, doesn't it? Common shares are the type you will start with because there are more of them than other types and because they are simple.

Buying stock in a company is different from buying bonds in the same company. When you buy a bond, you are lending the company money and it will pay you back with interest. When you buy stock, you are buying a piece of the company and no one has to pay you back if money runs short. You are an owner. Your return depends on the strength of the company.

If you can't be sure you'll get your money back, why would you even consider buying stock? The answer is you have a chance to make more money with stock than with bonds. As an owner, if the company makes a lot of money, you get part of it—a part equal to the size of the piece of pie, or number of shares, you own. The possibility of making a big return on your investment is why people are willing to risk some of their savings with stock purchases. Whether you can handle that possibility has to do with your risk tolerance.

When you buy stock, you sometimes get the benefit of stock splits. If a company is doing really well, the price of a share usually goes way up. This is because a lot of people want to buy shares in a successful company and few of the shareholders want to sell when their investment is doing so well. It's like when you have something that someone wants to buy, but you really like it and you won't sell unless you get a lot more money than you paid for it.

When the price of a stock goes up so high that a lot of people can't afford to buy a share, the company will sometimes do a *stock split*—it will split your shares in half or in thirds. This means you will have two or three shares for every share you owned before the split. This does not mean, however, that you suddenly have two or three times the amount of money you did before the split. That's because the price of each share is also cut in half or thirds. But after the split, the price of your shares usually continues to go up. Then you have more money than you did before the split, because now you own more shares.

Keeping Track of Your Stock

When you're a shareholder, the company sends you information about what it's doing. Shareholders get reports in the mail every three months or so. These reports are really just report cards, like those you get in school. In the case of stocks, the report tells you what the company has accomplished since it last contacted you. Once a year you get a report about what happened during the whole year. The report includes a written statement from the president of the company and information about how much money the company made for the year, how much it spent, and how much was left over to give to the shareholders. That's you.

The reports from the company help you figure out if the investment is living up to what you expected. Then you can decide if you want to keep your shares, sell them, or buy more shares. It boils down to the answer to this question: Are you making enough money to take the risk of owning stock? If no, then sell. If yes, then *hold* (that's a market term that means stay with what you have). If yes *big time*, then buy more.

It's time to mention risk tolerance again. People who invest only in stock need to have a higher tolerance for risk than those who invest only in bonds. That's because there is a greater chance of losing money with stock than there is with bonds, but at the same time, there is a greater chance of making money. Each person has to decide what she is comfortable doing with her savings. As I'm sure you've heard a thousand times, you have to try something before you know whether you like it or not.

The key to stock and bond investments is that you can make more money when you take bigger risks. Lion tamers make more than circus clowns, and high steel construction workers make more than carpenters because there's more risk. It's the same with investments. You will make more money with stocks than you will with bonds because there's more risk.

Find a Stock Report

Find a stock report. Ask your parents if they own any stocks or stock funds. If they do, ask to see one of the company's annual reports. If your parents don't own stock or mutual funds, ask your grandparents. If that doesn't work, go to the local library and ask the librarian if the library has any stock reports on file. If that doesn't work, look in the *Yellow Pages* of the phone book under "Brokers." Call one of the names that you find there and ask if she has a stock report she can mail you. If the office is close to where you live, ask if you can stop by and look at a number of reports. Explain to her why you are asking and she should be helpful.

When you find a report, look it over to see the various sections and different kinds of information the report includes. Read the president's report. You don't have to understand every word. Can you tell from this report if it was a good year for the business? Do you find any evidence in the report itself to back up what the president's report claims? The goal is to know what an annual report of a business company looks like, but if you can understand some of the information, this is even better. After reading the report would you buy stock in this company?

Mutual Funds

There's another way to invest your money and that is to buy shares in a mutual fund. A *mutual fund* is a company that invests money for you. Mutual funds come in all shapes and varieties. In fact, there are more than 5,000 mutual funds available. There are mutual funds that just sell treasury bonds. There are funds that just sell municipal bonds, and ones that just sell corporate bonds. There are also funds that just sell shares in stock companies. There are mutual funds that only sell stock in companies that have been around for a while, and there are funds that just sell stock in newer companies. There are mutual funds that just sell stock in big companies and funds that just sell stock in small companies. Almost anything you can think of that has to do with investments has a mutual fund of its own. The important thing for you to know about mutual funds is that you don't have to be a big investor to buy shares in one.

This is how a mutual fund works. One or two people pick out a group of stocks or bonds to go into a mutual fund that has a specific investment goal. The goal of the fund might be to make a lot of

There are a lot of words that investors use to mean investment earnings. Return, as in "steady return," is similar to the word interest. *Interest* means the money you are paid for the use of your money. *Return* also refers to the money you earn on an investment. *Yield* is another one. You will hear statements like, "My fund returned 10%." Or, "The yield on the fund was 10%." Both sentences mean the same thing. I guess it's just like *sweet* and *the bomb* and *neat* and *cool* and *groovy* and *phat*—these words all mean something's great.

money quickly, or it might be to invest money for a steady return—that means you can be pretty sure you'll get your money back with interest. The group of stocks or bonds that go in the fund is called a *portfolio*. The one or two people who pick what stocks and bonds to buy and sell are called *portfolio managers*.

Portfolio managers pick out a group of stocks or bonds that meet a certain goal and then they sell you shares in it. You already know that treasuries come in big denominations. Well, municipal bonds do, too—usually $5,000 a bond. But if you buy shares of a mutual fund, you can invest in treasuries or municipal bonds for as little as $1,000. What you are doing is buying a part (a share) of a treasury bond or a municipal bond. After you make your first purchase, you often can invest as little as $25 at a time in a mutual fund.

Besides making it easy for you to invest in a group of stocks or bonds, mutual funds cut down the risk of investing in stock. Here's how: when you buy shares in a mutual fund, you buy a tiny part of each of the stocks or bonds that the portfolio manager has put in the fund. If one of the stocks or bonds doesn't pay off as you had hoped, you won't lose all of your money. You will lose only a tiny part, as long as all the other stocks or bonds in the fund are still fine. For example, say you bought a fund that invested just in soft drinks like Coca-Cola, Pepsi, Mountain Dew, Canada Dry, and XYZola. XYZola has some problems. It goes bankrupt and the fund loses a little money, but all the other soft drinks are selling like crazy. You consequently did not lose all your money. In fact, you only lost a small portion of your money. What mutual funds do is help you to diversify your risk. To *diversify* simply means to spread out your risk. It's like when you play dodge ball—the more people who play, the less risk there is that you'll be the first one out.

On the other hand, if you had purchased shares in the XYZola Company alone and it went bankrupt, you would have lost your whole investment. Gone. That's a good reason why you should invest in some mutual funds at this stage in your investment career. You should still invest in some stocks. Just don't put all of your money in one thing.

$ Think of Ways to Earn Money

Write down five ways that you could earn money. Think about all the things you are good at. Is it reading out loud, or sewing, or yard work, or cleaning? Could you run errands for older people? Do you have elderly neighbors or grandparents who might have chores that you could do for them? Are there things your parents need to have done, like cleaning out the garage, getting the oil stains off the cement, or staining the deck before winter? Is there a veterinarian near you who would pay you to clean out cages and feed the animals on weekends? Use your imagination.

Next, follow up on at least one idea. First check with an adult in your house. He or she might have some thing that needs to be done right away. Put the money you earn aside in case you need to spend some money on supplies like a lawn mower or car wax. Work down the list. The job you find may not be your first choice, but just think how much fun it will be to have enough money to invest.

Billy Ray Invests in Himself and Starts a Small Business

Billy Ray was good at basketball, so instead of getting a full-time summer job while he was in high school, he went to basketball camp. He still did odd jobs, but mostly he practiced basketball. His family saw it as an investment in Billy Ray's college education. This investment paid off. Billy Ray went to Georgetown College in Georgetown, Kentucky, on a full basketball scholarship and never had to take out a student loan to help pay for his education.

Remember that Billy Ray had been paying himself when he did odd jobs during the school year, tucking half of that money into his savings account. In the early spring of his sophomore year in college, when he was 19, Billy Ray decided he had to do something with his summers to earn more money to save.

Winter has always been his brainstorming time. He says his mind works best when it's dark outside. So he started talking to people about jobs. One of those people he talked to had supported himself in college by starting a mowing company. Billy Ray decided that was a good choice for him, too.

He did some research to find out the things he needed to do to start his own mowing company. Billy Ray found used equipment in nearby Lexington. His

The Legend

Photo courtesy of Billy Ray Fawns

dad bought him a trailer to haul a mower, a weed eater, and a blower. He figured out how many lawns he would have to mow, and for how many months, to pay for the rest of the equipment. Then he walked into a bank—the same one where he had saved his money since he was eight. He asked the bank for a small business loan to buy the equipment he needed. He explained his mowing business idea, and how he planned to pay them back. He filled out the loan forms, and the bank reviewed them and decided to give Billy Ray the loan. He was off and running.

Billy Ray figured it would take a full year to pay off the loan. He paid it off in two months. During this period, as the number of people who wanted him to do their lawns increased, he realized he needed better equipment. So he went back to the bank and got another small business loan. He paid this one off the first month of his second summer. Now he owned his equipment free and clear. That meant that everything he made from mowing from then on was profit and could be invested. He had the money, now he just needed to learn how to invest it.

In this chapter you learned the major ways that investors invest and grow their savings. You learned about:

- risk tolerance
- savings bonds
- treasuries, and the different types of treasury bonds
- municipal bonds
- corporate bonds
- stocks
- mutual funds
- risk levels of each type of investment and the investment choices best suited to you, depending on your level of risk tolerance

Now it's time to find out how you actually make an investment, and where you go to do it.

Four

All About the Market

WHAT IS IT, AND WHERE IS WALL STREET?

Wall Street

NOW THAT YOU know what shares of stock are, it's time to talk about where you buy them and what you do when you get there. The place to start is on Wall Street.

The history of Wall Street is almost as interesting as the history of money. Wall Street is located in New York City at the southern end of the island of Manhattan. Manhattan is one of the oldest parts of the city. You've probably heard the story about how it was purchased from the

Lenape Native Americans in 1626 for the equivalent of about $24. Peter Minuit, a Dutchman, gave the Native Americans who lived and hunted there a few bead necklaces and trinkets in exchange for the land.

But there's another part of the story that you don't usually hear about. That's about the Dutch giving New York, or New Amsterdam as it was called then, to the English. Well, they didn't exactly give Manhattan to the English. They actually traded Manhattan to the English for a tiny island called Run Island, located in the East Indian Ocean. Run is so tiny that hardly anyone knew how to get there; however, it was worth its weight in gold because of a special tree that grew there—a nutmeg tree. Although nutmeg is used mostly in cakes and cookies and Swedish pancakes now, back then it was used for medicine. Everyone wanted nutmeg, so not only was the island of Run worth its weight in gold, it was also worth Manhattan to the Dutch.

Wall Street is a short street in the oldest part of Manhattan. It was named for a wall. Surprised? A fort was built near the edge of the island, and outside the fortress wall was a buttonwood tree. Starting as early as 1792, people started meeting under this tree to trade shares of stock. Pretty soon more and more people were meeting under the buttonwood tree. Finally they couldn't all fit, so they met anywhere along the street by the fortress wall that they could. Because Wall Street was so short, stock traders that got there late had to meet under other trees, or on the curb in front of buildings, or anywhere they could find. Before long the whole area around Wall Street was called Wall Street, no matter what street traders met on. Now, "Wall Street" means New York's financial district, where investors buy and sell stock.

Stock Exchanges

Trading on Wall Street doesn't take place under the buttonwood tree or on curbs anymore. Now it takes place in buildings and is done through companies called stock exchanges or stock markets. These companies are like huge supermarkets where you can buy, sell, or exchange almost anything—sort of like a Super K. Although there are numerous stock exchanges and stock markets around the country—including exchanges in Boston, Chicago, Los Angeles, and Philadelphia—the three biggest are on Wall Street.

New York Stock Exchange (NYSE)

The most famous of these three Wall Street exchanges is the New York Stock Exchange. Originally it was called the Buttonwood Group—because of the investors who met under the buttonwood tree. Now it's often referred to by the letters NYSE. The NYSE is the major place investors go to trade shares of big, established companies that make big, established products like cars, stoves, refrigerators, computers, and cameras.

The floor of the NYSE—where stocks are bought and sold—is one of the noisiest places in America. It's amazing to watch the traders yelling and screaming and jumping up and down, trying to be sure someone sees that they are buying or selling something. Just imagine a state basketball tournament with all the noisy fans and cheerleaders from both teams. Now imagine 10 teams and their fans on the court all at once. If you can do that, you will come close to knowing what one of the exchanges looks and sounds like.

National Association of Securities Dealers Automated Quotation (NASDAQ)

There is also a market for smaller, newer companies that make things like medicine, computer software, and other technological inventions. This market is called the NASDAQ Stock Market. NASDAQ stands for National Association of Securities Dealers Automated Quotation system. It's a long name, but all you need to remember is "NASDAQ,"—which rhymes with *has sack*.

The NASDAQ is different than the New York Stock Exchange because all the trades are done electronically over computers, instead of by yelling and jumping up and down to get noticed. Investors can buy or sell stocks on the NASDAQ exchange from anywhere in the world. In fact, investors who trade through the NASDAQ were probably the first of the on-line shoppers. Although the NASDAQ has more stocks listed for trade than the NYSE, the NYSE is still considered the granddaddy of the stock exchanges.

In late December 1999 and early January 2000, the NASDAQ opened a video tower and studio on Times Square in New York City. The tower is the largest video screen in the world. People can stand on the corner of Broadway and 43rd Street and watch news about the stock market all day long if they want. The NASDAQ's MarketSite Studio is a broadcast studio with 96 video screens to help reporters with their market update broadcasts. Since the tower is glass, you can also watch everything that's going on in the building. Find a TV channel that gives business news. If the reporter is standing in front of a lot of screens with charts, she is probably at the NASDAQ studio.

American Stock Exchange (AMEX)

The third major stock exchange is the American Stock Exchange or AMEX. It is the smallest of the three markets, and it used to be called the New York Curb Exchange. (Remember how stock trades would take place on the curbs up and down Wall Street?) The AMEX sells stocks of both large and small companies, but it has the fewest number of stocks to trade of the three exchanges. If you hear of someone referring to "the Curb," he means the American Stock Exchange. (There's a great trivia question for you!) In 1998, the AMEX merged with the NASDAQ, but the AMEX still operates as a separate market.

Over-the-Counter Market (OTC)

There's one more market that you should know about. It's called the over-the-counter market, or OTC. It really isn't a market like the big three markets. It's more like a flea market or yard sale. It's for all the stocks that are too new and too small to be listed on one of the major exchanges. The name for over-the-counter trading comes from an actual process. Originally, stock certificates were traded by handing them over a counter in a firm where brokers bought and sold stock for investors. Now the OTC market should be called the "over-the-phone" or "over-the-computer" market, since that's the way most of these tiny stocks are traded. In fact, some of the newer company stocks are so small that they are traded for pennies a share. If you ever read about penny stocks, the OTC market is where you usually buy them.

Some stocks trade over-the-counter so infrequently that it's hard to find out anything about them. There are two places where you can get information on what it costs to buy or sell one of these stocks. One is called the Pink Sheets (because it's printed on pink paper) and it's published by the OTC Bulletin Board. It lists stocks that are registered with the Securities and Exchange Commission (covered later in this chapter). Some stocks are so new and so small that they aren't even registered. The National Quotation Bureau puts out lists of these. You may want to check into penny stocks for your investment portfolio.

Visit a Stock Exchange

Now that you know there are stock exchanges in New York and other major cities, it's time to visit one. If you live in New York City, arrange a visit to the NYSE or to "the Curb," or you can just go to the corner of Broadway and 43rd Street and watch the NASDAQ video that shows current stock prices. If you visit the NASDAQ MarketSite Studio, you can play an interactive investing game or you can walk through the Information Tunnel to see what the global stock market is like.

If you live in Boston, Chicago, Cincinnati, Los Angeles, or Philadelphia, visit the exchanges in these cities. You might do this with your parents, or perhaps you could talk your teacher into planning a field trip to one of the exchanges. Each exchange has a viewing area and most of them offer guided tours.

Here is the stock exchange contact information:

New York Stock Exchange (NYSE)
11 Wall Street
New York, NY 10005
(212) 656-3000
www.nyse.com

NASDAQ MarketSite Studio (NASDAQ)
4 Times Square
New York, NY 10004
(212) 728-8333
www.nasdaq.com

The American Stock Exchange (AMEX)
86 Trinity Place
New York, NY 10006
(212) 306-1000
www.amex.com

Boston Stock Exchange, Inc. (BE)
1 Boston Place
38th Floor
Boston, MA 02108
(617) 723-9500
www.bostonstock.com

The Chicago Stock Exchange (CHX)
440 South LaSalle Street
Chicago, IL 60605
(312) 663-2222
www.chicagostockex.com

The Chicago Board Options Exchange (CBOE)
400 South LaSalle Street
Chicago, IL 60605
(312) 786-5600
www.cboe.com

The Cincinnati Stock Exchange (CSE)
440 South LaSalle Street
Chicago, IL 60605
(312) 786-8803
www.cincinnatistock.com

Pacific Stock Exchange, Inc. (PSE)
233 South Beaudry Avenue
12th Floor
Los Angeles, CA 90012
(213) 977-4500
www.pacificex.com

Philadelphia Stock Exchange (PHLX)
1900 Market Street
Philadelphia, PA 19103
(215) 496-5000
www.phlx.com

If you don't live near any of these cities that have exchanges—or even if you do—there's a great documentary on the history of Wall Street available on videotape, titled *The Great Game*. If your local library doesn't have a copy of this, you may purchase the video by sending a request and a $25 check to:

Burrelle's Transcripts
P.O. Box 7
Livingston, NJ 07039
(800) 777-8398

The Market

Now that you know where the stock exchanges are located, let's learn about how they work. The stock market is a lot like your local soccer league or a major baseball league. There are teams, players, and rules. To have a good season, everyone has to work together.

Here's how it happens. First, there are the stock exchanges, which are like sports leagues. These are where the shares of stock are traded, just as team members are sometimes traded to other teams. Then, there are the brokerage houses or firms, which are like team owners. Each firm is an investment company that is a member of the stock exchange. The brokerage firm pays the stock exchange to have what it calls "a seat" on the exchange. When a brokerage firm has a seat, it can buy or sell stocks through the exchange.

Each brokerage house hires stockbrokers—sometimes just called brokers. They are the players. Brokers are trained to advise investors about the best stock or bond buys, and to take care of either buying or selling stock for you on the stock exchange. Just like major league players, the best brokers get the biggest salaries.

The Birth of the Dow

In 1884, Charles Dow, a young journalist working in New York City, decided to make a list of 11 stocks that traded on the New York Stock Exchange. He thought that the 11 he picked, such as railroads and manufacturing companies, reflected America's wealth. Each day he wrote down the closing price for a share of each of the stocks, added them all together, and divided them by 11 to get the average. Sometimes he even published his list.

Before long, Dow joined forces with Edward Jones, another journalist who, like Dow, reported on business news. The two of them founded the *Wall Street Journal*, which regularly published this list called the Dow Jones Industrial Average (DJIA) or "the Dow." The *Wall Street Journal* is now the most important business-only newspaper in the United States—and maybe the world. Every day this business newspaper publishes a list of stocks and their average price. The DJIA is used around the world as an indication of the strength of America's stock market. The stocks in the Dow are not the same ones that Charles Dow started with, and more were added, but the concept is still the same. The Dow still follows big, well-established companies like Boeing, Coca-Cola, Disney, and McDonald's. These stocks even have a nickname—"blue-chip" stocks, named for the poker chips with the highest value.

The process of buying or selling the stock is actually called writing a ticket. When you buy a ticket to a baseball game, part of the cost of the ticket goes to the team owner to cover his costs and part of it goes to the player in salary. The same thing happens with brokers' commissions—part of the commission goes to the brokerage house to cover costs and the rest goes to the broker in salary. The broker who writes the most tickets makes the most money.

The Securities and Exchange Commission (often referred to as the SEC or the Commission) sets the rules for the stock and bond markets. Think of the SEC as the baseball commissioner. The SEC makes sure the broker tells you everything you need to know to make a reasonable investment decision, and then sends you a stock receipt on time. If the broker doesn't send your purchase documents or mishandles your purchase, the SEC investigates the reasons and sets penalties. If a broker is in trouble with the SEC, he may not be able to make stock or bond trades any more, plus he may have to pay a huge fine—hundreds of thousands of dollars—and even go to jail.

The Scoreboard

There's an easy way to check a scoreboard for the stock market each day. It's by looking at the ending numbers for the Dow Jones Industrial Average or the NASDAQ Composite Index. There are other stock indexes, like the Standard & Poor's 500 or the Russell 2000 Small Stock Index, but the Dow Jones Industrial Average and the NASDAQ are the ones you hear about most often.

The word *average* is probably familiar to you. You hear it in school a lot, as in "grade point average" or "average reading scores for the eighth grade." You also know sports terms such as "batting average." These are quick ways to compare students or athletes. The term *index* is another word that gives you a quick way to make these comparisons, such as comparing today against yesterday or a year ago.

The Dow Jones Industrial Average shows how 30 stocks that trade on the New York Stock Exchange sold for the day. It tells you whether, as a group, the value of the stock shares went up or down.

All the indexes work the same way. They measure share prices with different types of stocks. The NASDAQ Composite Index gives a quick look at new companies and technical stocks. The Russell 2000 follows small companies. The key is that when you hear the Dow mentioned on the news as going up or dropping a certain number of points for the day, it indicates that the stock market gained or lost value.

Find a Stockbroker

See if there are any stockbrokers in your community. Check in the *Yellow Pages* of your phone book under "Stock and Bond Brokers" to see if there are any brokerage houses listed. I checked in the phone book for Mount Sterling, Kentucky, where Billy Ray lives. Even though there were only 5,235 people living in Mount Sterling, there were listings for six brokerage firms!

How many are there in your town? If you have access to the *Yellow Pages* on the Internet, check the town where your grandparents live, the one where your sister goes to college, or just check any town or city that comes to mind. How many of the same brokerage house names show up in each town? Names like Paine Webber, Edward

Jones, and Merrill Lynch are some of the biggest and best-known bro-kerage houses. They're just like the Red Sox, the Yankees, and the Cubs—everybody knows these teams.

How to Place a Stock Order

To be able to play any kind of sport, you have to understand how the game works. You also have to know what the words mean that the coaches and other players use. The same is true with investing. I'll review a few important terms for you, so that at the end of this chapter you'll know how to place an order.

When you call a broker to buy or sell stock, you *place an order*. There are a number of things you need to know before you make that call:

- The name of the stock you want to buy or sell

- The class of the stock, whether the stock shares are common or preferred. (A *common* share is a regular type of share that most people have. A *preferred* share is one with extras, such as being one of the first stockholders to be paid dividends if there's a money crunch. The difference is sort of like hot fudge sundaes with or without whipped cream and nuts.)

- How many shares you want to buy or sell

- What you will pay or want to be paid for a particular stock (called setting the price)

The first three things are pretty straightforward. The fourth thing, however, means you have to know the lingo.

The simplest way to set the price, and the way most people do it, is to place a *market order*. A market order means that you will buy or sell your stock at the current market price. It's the same as going into a store to buy a pair of jeans. You walk straight to the shelves, find the style and size you want, and walk to the checkout counter to pay for them at the price marked on the sales tag. You want the jeans, you buy them, and there's no wait. It's the same way with stocks—if you place a market order, the trade is finished almost at once.

There are, however, two other ways to place an order. You can place a stop order or you can place a limited order. Both orders set limits on the price you are willing to pay (buy) or will accept for (sell) your stock. A *stop order* tells the broker to buy or sell a stock the moment the market price hits the price you set. A *limited order* is similar to a stop order, but there's one difference. A limited order allows the broker to sell your stock at an even better price than you indicated, if someone offers more than you expected; or, if you can buy it at a lower price than you were willing to pay, then the broker can save you money on your original order.

Here's how it works. You decide you want to purchase 10 shares of VideoKids stock, because you always have to wait in a long checkout line when you're ready to pay. This personal experience tells you that it's a popular place. You look in the paper and find that VideoKids traded for $10 a share yesterday, but that over the last 52 weeks it has sometimes traded as low as $8 a share. (I'll explain how to check this out in the next chapter.) You decide that you are willing to buy the stock at $9 a share. You ask the adult who handles your stock purchases to place a stop order to buy 10 shares of VideoKids stock at $9 a share. When you place either a stop or a limited order, the broker will ask if you want a day order or a good until cancelled order (GTC). If you answer that you want a *day order*, the order will be open until the stock market closes trading on that very day. If you answer that you want a *good until cancelled order*, your order will be open until it's filled or until you cancel it. To *fill an order* simply means to buy or sell the stock you want. So, if your order is filled, it means you bought 10 shares of VideoKids at $9 a share. You then pay the broker $90 (10 shares x $9) plus the broker's commission.

You sell stock shares exactly the same way. Let's say that your Kidstech.com stock has spiked up and down over the last year. You bought it at $18 a share and the stock has traded as high as $26 a share. When you check the paper, you see that yesterday the stock traded at $20. You decide to sell your shares if you can get $22 a share. So you place a stop order with the broker to sell all of your Kidstech.com shares when the stock hits $22 a share. You also tell the broker that your order is good for 30 days, which means that you are willing to wait 30 days to see if it sells. If Kidstech.com does not reach $22 a share in 30 days, the broker will contact you and ask if you want to cancel your order or keep it open. Then you can decide if you want to keep the stock or place a GTC order. It's that simple. Just as you're comfortable with the terms *strike*, *out*, and *safe* in baseball, soon you'll feel the same way about the terms *market*, *stop*, and *GTC orders*.

How to Place a Mutual Fund Order

Mutual funds are made up of individual stocks, but placing a mutual fund order is a lot easier than placing a stock order. The main reason is that you don't have to know any terms except *buy* and *sell*. To place an order for mutual funds, you call the mutual fund company that manages the fund you want. This is all you have to say: "I want to buy $500 of your KidsScene Fund," or, "I want to buy 50 shares of your KidsScene Fund." The person who takes the call will ask if you have an account with the mutual fund company. If this is your first purchase, he will mail you a short form to fill out. You send it back with your check or money order to purchase the stock and it's done. The mutual fund family will even send you a form that lets you add money—say $25—to your fund whenever you want to. All you have to do is send the form back with a check or money order made out to the name of the fund. When you want to sell, you just call the fund company and say you want to sell a certain amount of your fund. You can do this in dollar amounts or in number of shares. It's as easy as that. In a few days you will receive a check in the mail for what you sold.

There are good reasons for buying mutual funds. I've described some of the reasons in Chapter 3. Some people, though, buy mutual funds only because they don't know how to place a stock order. They are afraid they'll sound dumb if they don't know exactly what to say. But you already know what to say, so you can buy either stock or mutual funds based on which is the best investment for you. Besides, you don't have to worry about what other people think. Remember, you're the one with the money to invest.

Write a Script

Write a script for a stock order. Pretend that you're going to buy 10 shares of stock in the company that makes your favorite shoes. Write out two scripts for the person who will place your order, one for placing a market order with a broker and one for placing a stop order. Finally, write out another script, pretending that you already own stock in the shoe company and you want to sell your shares. Decide if you want it to be a stop or a limited order and adjust your script. Decide if you want it to be a day order or a GTC order and add this into the script, too.

Billy Ray Plans to Invest

Billy Ray thinks through each of his decisions carefully. He figured that in the second summer of his mowing business he'd be able to save most of what he made. So he started going around and asking adults, "Looking back, if you were my age, what would you do with your money now that you didn't do then?" He listened carefully to what everyone had to say and collected all the information. He researched different types of investments that were mentioned, made his decisions, and formed a plan.

He decided to divide his savings into thirds—one third was for high-risk investments, one third was for medium-risk investments, and the last third was for low-risk investments. He figured out which investments were best for him, and then he made his move.

In this chapter the stock market was introduced to you. You learned:
- that the history of Wall Street began under a buttonwood tree
- how the market works
- that there are different stock exchanges
- that when investors buy or sell stock, they contact a stockbroker

- that stockbrokers work for a brokerage house, and the brokerage house is a member of one or all of the stock exchanges
- how you can get a quick look at how well stocks did for the day by looking at the Dow Jones Industrial Average

Next you'll learn how to research the stocks that you're interested in.

All About Stock Tables

HOW TO READ THEM FOR FUN AND MONEY

How to Read Stock Tables

YOU KNOW THE terminology and how the market works, but before you actually place an order, you have to decide what you're going to buy. This is the next step in the investment process. It's kind of like a detective game. You try to learn all you can about a stock from just a few clues. After you learn how to read the clues, picking the right stock becomes a piece of cake.

The good news is that these clues are at your fingertips in your local newspaper. There are pages of information called *stock tables*. Reading the stock tables is something that a lot of grown-ups don't know how to do, and many are scared to even try. By the end of this chapter you'll be able to show them how to do it. Once you know what to look for, they're really easy to read.

A stock table tells you the recent history of a stock, just like statistics on the sports page tell you how well a baseball player has done over the season. There are two main reasons you need to understand these tables. One is to see how the stocks you own are doing. The other is to see how stocks you might want to buy have done in the past. This will help you decide if you want to buy shares in a particular company. There's actually one more good reason to learn how to read the stock tables—so you'll never be afraid to use them. If you aren't afraid, then you won't be slowed down when you want to invest. It's like learning how to ride a bike—once you know how to do it, you never even have to think about it again. You just get on and ride. The only difference is that learning to read stock tables is a lot easier than learning how to ride a bike.

Here's an example. Let's say that you hear on television that Disney has made a new film that will open around the holidays. You think Disney might be a good stock to own, but you don't have a clue about what it costs per share. The quickest way to find out is to check the stock tables. Although you can use the Internet to find information on stocks, one of the easiest ways is to check in a newspaper. If you live in a large city like New York or Chicago, stock tables are published every day. If you live in a smaller town, stock tables may be published only once a week; but even

1/16	1/8	3/16	1/4	5/16
.625	.125	.1875	.25	.3125
6	13	19	25	31

3/8	7/16	1/2	9/16	5/8
.375	.4375	.50	.5625	.625
38	44	50	56	63

11/16	3/4	13/16	7/8	15/16
.6875	.75	.8125	.875	.9375
69	75	81	88	94

Before you read a stock table, you have to know something about how the numbers are published. In the table shown here the prices are listed in fractions, but soon the prices will all be listed in decimals—that means in dollars and cents. Just in case you run into fractions in the future, here's what each fraction equals in decimals and pennies.

in a small town, the local library will have the *New York Times* or a financial newspaper that includes the daily stock tables. You'll find the stock tables printed in the business section of the paper.

Disney

Now back to Disney. Since Disney is a big company, I looked first for the stock under the list of stocks that trade on the New York Stock Exchange. It was there. If it had not been there, I would have looked under the NASDAQ National Market and then under the American Stock Exchange list. Notice that the stocks are listed alphabetically, and that across the top of each table are headings in dark letters for each column. (You can see these on the previous page.) Reading them from left to right they are: "52-Week High, Low, Stock," and so on. Most newspapers have

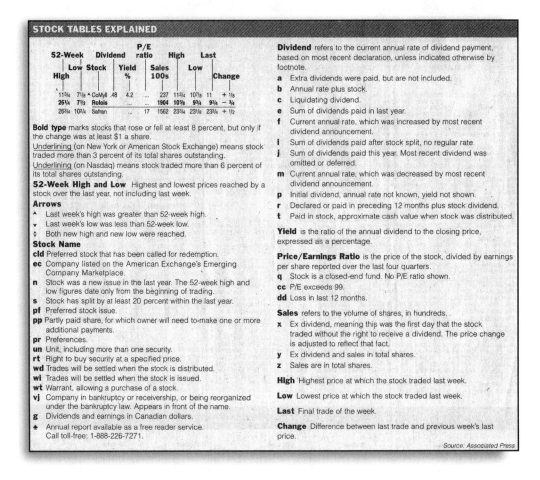

STOCK TABLES EXPLAINED

52-Week High	52-Week Low	Stock	Dividend Yield %	P/E ratio	Sales 100s	High	Low	Last	Change
11¾	7⅛ ▲	CoMyll	.48	4.2	...	237	11¾	10⅞	11	+ ⅛
26¼	7½	Rolois	...	...	1904	10⅝	9¾	9¾	− ¾
26¾	10¾	Safran	...	17	1562	23¾	23⅛	23¾	+ ½

Bold type marks stocks that rose or fell at least 8 percent, but only if the change was at least $1 a share.

Underlining (on New York or American Stock Exchange) means stock traded more than 3 percent of its total shares outstanding.

Underlining (on Nasdaq) means stock traded more than 6 percent of its total shares outstanding.

52-Week High and Low Highest and lowest prices reached by a stock over the last year, not including last week.

Arrows

▲ Last week's high was greater than 52-week high.

▼ Last week's low was less than 52-week low.

⬍ Both new high and new low were reached.

Stock Name

cld Preferred stock that has been called for redemption.

ec Company listed on the American Exchange's Emerging Company Marketplace.

n Stock was a new issue in the last year. The 52-week high and low figures date only from the beginning of trading.

s Stock has split by at least 20 percent within the last year.

pf Preferred stock issue.

pp Partly paid share, for which owner will need to make one or more additional payments.

pr Preferences.

un Unit, including more than one security.

rt Right to buy security at a specified price.

wd Trades will be settled when the stock is distributed.

wi Trades will be settled when the stock is issued.

wt Warrant, allowing a purchase of a stock.

vj Company in bankruptcy or receivership, or being reorganized under the bankruptcy law. Appears in front of the name.

g Dividends and earnings in Canadian dollars.

♣ Annual report available as a free reader service. Call toll-free: 1-888-226-7271.

Dividend refers to the current annual rate of dividend payment, based on most recent declaration, unless indicated otherwise by footnote.

a Extra dividends were paid, but are not included.

b Annual rate plus stock.

c Liquidating dividend.

e Sum of dividends paid in last year.

f Current annual rate, which was increased by most recent dividend announcement.

i Sum of dividends paid after stock split, no regular rate.

j Sum of dividends paid this year. Most recent dividend was omitted or deferred.

m Current annual rate, which was decreased by most recent dividend announcement.

p Initial dividend, annual rate not known, yield not shown.

r Declared or paid in preceding 12 months plus stock dividend.

t Paid in stock, approximate cash value when stock was distributed.

Yield is the ratio of the annual dividend to the closing price, expressed as a percentage.

Price/Earnings Ratio is the price of the stock, divided by earnings per share reported over the last four quarters.

q Stock is a closed-end fund. No P/E ratio shown.

cc P/E exceeds 99.

dd Loss in last 12 months.

Sales refers to the volume of shares, in hundreds.

x Ex dividend, meaning this was the first day that the stock traded without the right to receive a dividend. The price change is adjusted to reflect that fact.

y Ex dividend and sales in total shares.

z Sales are in total shares.

High Highest price at which the stock traded last week.

Low Lowest price at which the stock traded last week.

Last Final trade of the week.

Change Difference between last trade and previous week's last price.

Source: Associated Press

a box inserted somewhere near the stock tables that explains what each of the headings mean. Sometimes you'll find a letter by the stock name or in the dividend column. These are also explained in the box. Here's what each heading means.

52-Week High The highest price that was paid for a share of stock in the last year (52 weeks). Sometimes you'll see an arrow pointing up in the 52-Week High column. That means that the selling price listed for the current day is the highest in the last 52 weeks.

52-Week Low The lowest price that was paid for a share of stock in the last year. Sometimes you'll see an arrow pointing down in the 52-Week Low column. That means that the selling price listed for the current day is the lowest in the last 52 weeks.

Stock The name of the stock. If the company name is short enough, like Disney or Benetton, then the full name is used. If the company name is long, like Barnes and Noble, then a shortened version is used. Barnes and Noble's shortened version is BarnNbl and, like this one, the name in the paper is usually close enough that you can find it.

Sym The company stock symbol. Some papers include a column for the stock symbol and some papers don't. Companies try to make their symbols close to their actual name (like OAT for Quaker Oats), but if there are a lot of names that are similar, then sometimes the symbols don't match up so well. If you're really curious and stuck about the meaning of an abbreviation, then you can call one of the brokers listed in Chapter 8 or check it out on-line.

Div The dividend, or the estimated amount that you will get per year in cash for each share that you own. If there is a blank under the Div column, it means the stock does not pay a dividend. (In this case, your investment return comes from an increase in the price of the stock.) Dividend is sometimes called yield. Remember that interest, dividend, yield, and return all mean money earned.

Yld % Percent yield. This is a clue about dividends. The percent yield tells you the dividend percent based on the price paid for the stock. In the case of Disney, the company expects to pay a dividend of .21 or 21 cents per share. On the day I'm using as an example, August 6, 2000, Disney sold for $42^7/_{16}$ or $42.44 a share. (Use the conversion table on page 57 and round to the nearest penny.) If you divide .21 by 42.44 you get 0.0049. (When you are dealing with percentages, you move the decimal point two numbers to the right. You end up with 0.49 or, rounded up, 0.5, which is what the stock table shows. Don't worry, you won't ever have to do this calculation yourself. I just wanted to explain how the table got this number. I knew someone once who worked through all of Einstein's calculations on relativity just so he would know for sure how it was done. It took him a year. But don't panic, you won't ever have to do that either.)

P/E The price to earnings ratio. This means the price divided by earnings. The price part of the equation is the price that the stock last sold at. The earnings part is the amount the company earned per share over the last year. The stock table does not supply us with the amount of earnings the company had over the previous four quarters or full year. The table simply gives the P/E ratio. What it tells you is how expensive, or "pricey," the stock is compared to what the company earned during the last year. It's sort of like paying $50 for a ticket to an unknown music group when you could see the hottest group around for the same price. The closer the price is to the earnings the better, so look for lower P/E ratios.

Sales 100s The amount of shares that changed hands on the last business day. The number is given in hundreds, which means you add two zeros to the back to see exactly how many shares sold. Sometimes the heading is "Vol 100s." That means the same thing. Here's a weird little twist: if there is a *Z* in front of the number, you don't have to add the zeros. If you see 1522 in the 100s column, that means 152,200 shares sold; but, if the number is Z1522, it means that only 1,522 shares were sold. If there is a line under the stock's entry it means that more shares than usual changed hands, and that usually means that there's some important news about the stock.

High The highest price paid for a share of stock for the day. Remember, the high on the left side of the table is the high for the year. If it's on the right, it's the high for the previous business day.

Low The lowest price paid for a share of stock for the previous business day. Again, the low on the left of the table is the low for the whole year.

Last The price of the last share sold for the previous business day. Sometimes this heading is "Close," which means the closing bell price and, consequently, the last price. This is usually the first column investors look at to see what their stock was worth at the end of the day. You'll hear it referred to in a number of ways, such as "closing price" or "market close."

Chg Change. This column gives you the amount of change between the previous day's closing price and the closing price from the day before that. There will always be a plus (+) or a minus (–) sign in the Change column to tell you whether the stock went up or down. (See the table for the meanings of other abbreviations.)

Disney from Start to Finish

Now let's look at Disney from start to finish. (Refer to the stock table on page 57.) You hear about this new movie coming out for the holidays and you want to see if you can afford to buy some Disney stock now. You also want to get a picture of how the stock has done over the last year, so you find a newspaper and check the New York Stock Exchange.

You look over to the right side of the columns, the column for "Last," to see what the stock price was at the end of the previous day. You see that it closed at $42^7/_{16}$ or $42.44 a share. You then check the next column to the right to see if it closed up or down from the day before. In this case, it was up $4^9/_{16}$ or $4.56 over the last day. That's good in one way. It means a lot of people think Disney is a good stock. But it's bad in another way, because you would rather pay less for the stock than more. If you had bought it on the day before the current listing, you would have saved more than $4.50 a share.

Now you look all the way over to the left edge of the table and you check to see what Disney's high and low prices have been for the last year. In the last 52 weeks, Disney shares sold for as low as $23^3/_8$ or $23.38 and as high as $43^7/_8$ or $43.88. Going back to the closing price on our table, you can see that Disney is currently selling near its high for the year. That's not so good. It means that Disney stock is pretty expensive right now. It also means that everyone who heard about the new film had the same idea as you, so all of them are buying the stock. You check the number of shares that sold in one day and you see that more than 36 million shares were sold. That's a lot of shares. (When a lot of people want the same thing, it means the seller can ask more because someone out there will want it badly enough to pay a higher price.)

The next question to ask is what kind of dividend you could expect to earn in a year for each share of stock you purchased. You see on the stock table that you would get 21 cents a share. So if you bought 10 shares, which would cost you $424.40 at the listed price, you would get about $2.10 in earnings for the year (10 x .21 = $2.10). Now you ask yourself how that dividend compares to other stocks. Disney's dividend compared to the stock price is 0.5%, which is low. If you look at the stocks above and below Disney, you see that most of them have a higher dividend percentage. One stock even gives dividends that are equal to 13.4% of the cost of a share of stock. Then you look at the price/earnings ratio—how much the price of a share is compared to the earnings for the last year. You see that Disney stock is selling for 85 times the amount of earnings the company made per share over the last four quarters. That's not good. That's too high.

Now you have the tools to make a decision. The decision to buy or not is often a hard one. It's hard because often your heart wants to do one thing and your head tells you something else. You would love to tell your friends that you own some shares of Disney stock. Then, each time Disney released a new film, you would feel really proud because you owned a part of the company. However (and this is the hard part) Disney stock is selling near its highest price for the last 52 weeks and its dividends are low compared to the price of the stock. Plus, what you would have to pay for the stock compared to the amount of money the company earned last year is too high. This means that Disney is not the best buy right now. So, even though you had a good idea when you heard about the new Disney film, and even though you would love to own some Disney shares, it's not a good investment at this time.

Some investors just buy what they want without doing their research, but that's like betting on a horse just because you like its name. Those horses rarely win. You'll come out a winner much more often if you do the research first and then make your decision based on what you find.

Pat yourself on the back, because you now have more than half of the tools you need to call yourself an informed investor!

$ Look Up Stocks

Look up the following stocks in the stock table of the most recent paper you can find: Nabisco, as in cookies; United, as in airlines; and Microsoft, as in software. Check all three exchanges to find these stock listings.

Now look up Disney. Fill in the bottom row of the table on the next page with the information for the new date.

Disney in August 2000 Compared to Today's Date					
52-Week High	52-Week Low	Stock	Div	Yld %	PE
$43^7/_8$	$23^3/_8$	Disney	.21	0.5	85

Disney in August 2000 Compared to Today's Date continued				
Sales 100s	High	Low	Last	Change
360736	43	38	$42^7/_{16}$	$+4^9/_{16}$

Compare the two sets of numbers and ask yourself the following questions:

- Does a share of Disney stock cost more or less today than it did in August 2000?

- What happened to the highs and lows for the last 52 weeks? Have they changed a lot or are they pretty much the same as before?

- Has the dividend changed?

- Has the price/earnings ratio gotten better or worse? (Better means the ratio is lower; worse means it's higher.) Remember that the price/earnings ratio gives you a comparison between the price of the stock and the company's last years' earnings. If the P/E ratio is high, it means that you are paying a lot for a stock that has low earnings.

- What about sales? Is the stock still as popular as it was in August 2000?

- Finally, would you have made money if you bought Disney stock in August 2000? Has the price gone up or down or is it about the same?

You just did a stock analysis. When you look up a stock in the stock tables, it gives you a picture of the stock for one day. It's a snapshot. When you check a stock once a week or once a month, you can see what a stock does over time. The kind of comparison you just did with Disney—looking at the stock over time—is closer to a video than a snapshot portrait of a company. This is exactly what brokers and financial advisors do every day. Did it ever occur to you that you could do it, too?

Go tell someone over age 18 some of the things you've just learned or show him or her how to look up a stock in the paper. You can use Disney if you want, since you know exactly where to find it. Do the same analysis for the other three companies: Nabisco, United, and Microsoft. Are any of these better investments than Disney at this time?

Reading Mutual Fund Tables

Now that you know how to read stock tables, you'll be able to read mutual fund tables, too. They're very similar. However, to make certain that you're as comfortable reading the mutual fund tables as the stock tables, I'm covering them separately here.

Remember that a mutual fund is simply a group of stocks or bonds selected by a portfolio manager. Investors buy shares in the fund, just like they do in a single stock. When you buy shares in a mutual fund, you own a part of each of the stock companies in the fund. Also, remember that mutual funds help you spread out your risk. (Refer to Chapter 3 if you need to review this information.)

As you can see from the following illustration, funds are listed under bolded names. This is the name of the investment company that manages the group of funds listed beneath it. The funds that a company manages are referred to as its family of funds. Each fund has a different investment objective. Some have low-risk levels and some have high-risk levels; some give you big dividends, and some don't give any dividends at all.

When you check on mutual funds in a daily newspaper, you see just a few columns:

Fund Family The name of the company that manages the mutual funds in its list.

Fund Name Placed right below the Fund Family heading, these are the names of the mutual funds. Each fund is managed by a portfolio manager and is designed to meet a certain goal, like giving the investor income through dividends, or like buying new companies that the manager thinks will grow and make a lot of money for investors.

NAV The net asset value, or what a share of the fund is worth and, consequently, what an investor has to pay for a share of the mutual fund. The NAV is also what an investor gets when he sells a share of the fund.

Dly % Ret. The daily percent return, or the amount the fund gained or lost in value from the NAV on the day before. The number will always have a plus (+) or minus (–) sign in front of it just as it does in the stock tables. (The percent change is calculated by subtracting the price you see in the newspaper from the price listed the day before and then dividing that number by the price listed the day before.) The table makes it really easy because it just gives you the percent change. You don't have to do the math yourself each time.

YTD % Ret. The year-to-date percent return, or the amount the fund has gained or lost since the beginning of the year. This number also will have a (+) or (–) sign in front of it and is calculated the same way as the daily percent return.

This is the mutual fund information you'll see most days when you check the paper or check for the mutual fund quotations on-line. Sometimes, at least once every three months starting on January 1, the funds provide investors with extra information called the Mutual Funds Quarterly Review. Here's what it looks like.

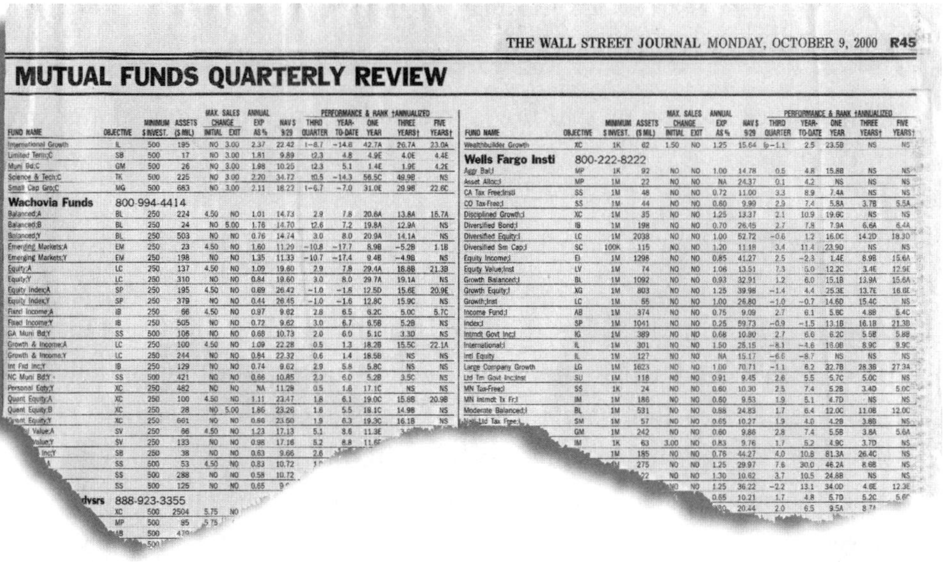

THE WALL STREET JOURNAL MONDAY, OCTOBER 9, 2000 R45

MUTUAL FUNDS QUARTERLY REVIEW

FUND NAME	OBJECTIVE	MINIMUM $ INVEST.	ASSETS ($ MIL)	MAX. SALES CHANGE INITIAL	EXIT	ANNUAL EXP AS %	NAV $ 9/29	PERFORMANCE & RANK †ANNUALIZED THIRD QUARTER	YEAR-TO-DATE	ONE YEAR	THREE YEARS†	FIVE YEARS†
International Growth	IL	500	195	NO	3.00	2.37	22.42	t−8.7	−14.6	42.7A	26.7A	23.0A
Limited Term;C	SB	500	17	NO	3.00	1.81	9.89	t2.3	4.8	4.9E	4.0E	4.4E
Muni Bd;C	GM	500	26	NO	3.00	1.98	10.25	t2.3	5.1	1.4E	1.9E	4.2E
Science & Tech;C	TK	500	225	NO	3.00	2.20	34.72	t0.5	−14.3	56.5C	49.9B	NS
Small Cap Gro;C	MG	500	683	NO	3.00	2.11	18.22	t−6.7	−7.0	31.0E	29.9B	22.6C
Wachovia Funds	800-994-4414											
Balanced;A	BL	250	224	4.50	NO	1.01	14.73	2.9	7.8	20.6A	13.8A	15.7A
Balanced;B	BL	250	24	NO	5.00	1.76	14.70	t2.6	7.2	19.8A	12.9A	NS
Balanced;Y	BL	250	503	NO	NO	0.76	14.74	3.0	8.0	20.9A	14.1A	NS
Emerging Markets;A	EM	250	23	4.50	NO	1.60	11.29	−10.8	−17.7	8.9B	−5.2B	1.1B
Emerging Markets;Y	EM	250	198	NO	NO	1.35	11.33	−10.7	−17.4	9.4B	−4.9B	NS
Equity;A	LC	250	137	4.50	NO	1.09	19.60	2.9	7.8	29.4A	18.8B	21.3B
Equity;Y	LC	250	310	NO	NO	0.84	19.60	3.0	8.0	29.7A	19.1A	NS
Equity Index;A	SP	250	195	4.50	NO	0.69	26.42	−1.0	−1.8	12.5D	15.6E	20.9E
Equity Index;Y	SP	250	379	NO	NO	0.44	26.45	−1.0	−1.6	12.8C	15.9C	NS
Fixed Income;A	IB	250	66	4.50	NO	0.97	9.62	2.8	6.5	6.2C	5.0C	5.7C
Fixed Income;Y	IB	250	505	NO	NO	0.72	9.62	3.0	6.7	6.5B	5.2B	NS
GA Muni Bd;Y	SS	500	106	NO	NO	0.68	10.73	2.0	6.0	5.1C	3.3D	NS
Growth & Income;A	LC	250	100	4.50	NO	1.09	22.28	0.5	1.3	18.2B	15.5C	22.1A
Growth & Income;Y	LC	250	244	NO	NO	0.84	22.32	0.6	1.4	18.5B	NS	NS
Int Fxd Inc;Y	IB	250	129	NO	NO	0.74	9.62	2.9	5.8	5.8C	NS	NS
NC Muni Bd;Y	SS	500	421	NO	NO	0.66	10.85	2.3	6.0	5.2B	3.5C	NS
Personal Eqty;Y	XC	250	482	NO	NO	NA	11.28	0.5	1.6	17.1C	NS	NS
Quant Equity;A	XC	250	100	4.50	NO	1.11	23.47	1.8	6.1	19.0C	15.8B	20.9B
Quant Equity;B	XC	250	28	NO	5.00	1.86	23.26	1.6	5.5	18.1C	14.9B	NS
Quant Equity;Y	XC	250	661	NO	NO	0.66	23.50	1.9	6.3	19.3C	16.1B	NS
Value;A	SV	250	66	4.50	NO	1.23	17.13	5.1	8.6	11.3E	3.	
Value;Y	SV	250	133	NO	NO	0.98	17.16	5.2	8.8	11.6		
Inc;Y	SB	250	38	NO	NO	0.63	9.66	2.6				
A	SS	500	53	4.50	NO	0.83	10.72	1.				
	SS	500	288	NO	NO	0.58	10.72					
	SS	500	125	NO	NO	0.65	9.					
dvsrs	888-923-3355											
	XC	500	2504	5.75	NO							
	MP	500	85	5.75								
	IB	500	47									
		500										

FUND NAME	OBJECTIVE	MINIMUM $ INVEST.	ASSETS ($ MIL)	MAX. SALES CHANGE INITIAL	EXIT	ANNUAL EXP AS %	NAV $ 9/29	PERFORMANCE & RANK †ANNUALIZED THIRD QUARTER	YEAR-TO-DATE	ONE YEAR	THREE YEARS†	FIVE YEARS†
Wealthbuilder Growth	XC	1K	62	1.50	NO	1.25	15.64	fp−1.1	2.5	23.5B	NS	NS
Wells Fargo Insti	800-222-8222											
Aggr Bal;I	MP	1K	92	NO	NO	1.00	14.78	0.5	4.8	15.8B	NS	NS
Asset Alloc;I	MP	1M	22	NO	NO	NA	24.37	0.1	4.2	NS	NS	NS
CA Tax Free;Instl	SS	1M	48	NO	NO	0.72	11.00	3.3	8.9	7.4A	NS	NS
CO Tax-Free;I	SS	1M	44	NO	NO	0.60	9.99	2.9	7.4	5.8A	3.7B	5.5A
Disciplined Growth;I	XC	1M	35	NO	NO	1.25	13.37	2.1	10.9	19.6C	NS	NS
Diversified Bond;I	IB	1M	198	NO	NO	0.70	26.45	2.7	7.8	7.9A	6.6A	6.4A
Diversified Equity;I	LC	1M	2038	NO	NO	1.00	52.72	−0.6	1.2	16.0C	14.2D	18.3D
Diversified Sm Cap;I	SC	100K	115	NO	NO	1.20	11.18	3.4	11.4	23.9D	NS	NS
Equity Income;I	EI	1M	1298	NO	NO	0.85	41.27	2.5	−2.3	1.4E	8.9B	15.6A
Equity Value;Inst	LV	1M	74	NO	NO	1.06	13.51	7.3	5.0	12.2C	3.4E	12.9E
Growth Balanced;I	BL	1M	1092	NO	NO	0.93	32.91	1.2	6.0	15.1B	13.9A	15.6A
Growth Equity;I	XG	1M	803	NO	NO	1.25	39.98	−1.4	4.4	25.3E	13.7E	16.6E
Growth;Inst	LC	1M	65	NO	NO	1.00	26.80	−1.0	−0.7	14.6D	15.4C	NS
Income Fund;I	AB	1M	374	NO	NO	0.75	9.09	2.7	6.1	5.6C	4.8B	5.4C
Index;I	SP	1M	1041	NO	NO	0.25	59.73	−0.9	−1.5	13.1B	16.1B	21.3B
Intmdt Govt Inc;I	IG	1M	389	NO	NO	0.68	10.80	2.7	6.6	6.2C	5.5B	5.8B
International;I	IL	1M	301	NO	NO	1.50	25.15	−8.1	−4.6	16.0B	8.9C	9.9C
Intl Equity	IL	1M	127	NO	NO	NA	15.17	−6.6	−8.7	NS	NS	NS
Large Company Growth	LG	1M	1623	NO	NO	1.00	70.71	−1.1	6.2	32.7B	28.3B	27.3A
Ltd Tm Govt Inc;Inst	SU	1M	118	NO	NO	0.91	9.45	2.6	5.5	5.7C	5.0C	NS
MN Tax-Free;I	SS	1K	24	NO	NO	0.60	10.30	2.5	7.4	5.2B	3.4D	5.0C
MN Intmdt Tx Fr;I	IM	1M	186	NO	NO	0.60	9.53	1.9	5.1	4.7D	NS	NS
Moderate Balanced;I	BL	1M	531	NO	NO	0.88	24.83	1.7	6.4	12.0C	11.0B	12.0C
Natl Ltd Tax Free;I	SM	1M	57	NO	NO	0.65	10.27	1.9	4.0	4.2B	3.8B	NS
	GM	1M	242	NO	NO	0.60	9.86	2.8	7.4	5.5B	3.8A	5.6A
	IM	1K	63	3.00	NO	0.83	9.76	1.7	5.2	4.9C	3.7D	NS
		1M	185	NO	NO	0.76	44.27	4.0	10.8	81.3A	26.4C	NS
			275	NO	NO	1.25	29.97	7.6	30.0	46.2A	8.6B	NS
			22	NO	NO	1.30	10.62	3.7	10.5	24.8B	NS	NS
				NO	NO	1.25	36.22	−2.2	13.1	34.0D	4.6E	12.3E
						0.65	10.21	1.7	4.8	5.7D	5.2C	5.6
							20.44	2.0	6.5	9.5A	8.7	

As you can see, some of the stuff we already talked about is in there. But there are some new columns, and they have very good information in them. There's one long heading called "Performance & Rank" (sometimes this is called "Total Return," but it means the same thing). Under the Performance & Rank heading are several columns with headings of their own. That's where the real clues are lurking. These columns tell you how much the fund gained (+) or lost (–) over a set period of time. The figures under the subheadings include all of the dividends you might have earned if you owned the fund for one, three, or five years and left your dividends to be reinvested. This is a lot like the power of compounding—you make more money on the money you already made.

You will also see a letter after the one-, three-, and five-year total return. (Sometimes a 10-year figure is included, too.) These letters are just like grades. They tell you how the fund compares to other funds of the same type. So, for example, if you see that a growth fund has an *A* in the ranking column, you know that it ranked in the top 20% of all growth funds in total return; if it has a *B* it's in the next 20% down, and so on until you get to the fateful *E*, which means the fund ranked with the worst funds for total return. If a fund has several *E*s, then you should stay away from it, but you probably figured that out already.

Sometimes these columns don't include numbers for a particular mutual fund; instead they have the abbreviation *NS*. This means that the fund did not exist during that time period. If there is an *NS*, it's usually under the five-year heading, but sometimes the fund is only one or two years old, so you see the *NS* in several of the columns.

Here are the meanings of the other columns:

Objective Refers to the types of stocks the fund usually buys. There are thousands of mutual funds, but each of those funds is supposed to fit under a specific category. There are 36 categories in all. There are gold funds that invest in gold mines and gold coins; there are Pacific Region funds that invest only in stocks of Japan, China, and other Asian countries; there are European funds that only buy stocks from Germany, France, and other European countries; there are health and biotechnology funds that invest only in companies that provide medicine and hospitals and things that have to do with health—and that's just the beginning. Each type of fund has two letters that identify the category it belongs to: Gold (AU); Pacific Region (PR); Europe (EU); Health and Biotechnology (HB). Two of the biggest selling categories are Growth funds (GR), which invest in smaller companies that look like they might grow bigger and get richer; and Growth and Income funds (GI), which invest in some companies that are expected to grow bigger and in other companies that already give steady dividends or income. There's a list of the meaning of each of these abbreviations included in the paper when these quarterly reviews appear.

MaxSalesCharge This is the maximum charge for placing an order. When brokers sell certain mutual funds, they get commissions just as they do when they sell stocks. With mutual funds it is called a sales charge or *load*, and the load comes out of what you paid for your shares of the fund. Many funds charge a maximum initial charge so they can pay the broker who sold it to you up front—or the minute you buy the fund. This is called an *up-front load*. You can compare the fees of different funds by comparing this number down the column with the heading "Initial." If zeros appear in this column, that means there is no initial charge or up-front load. The funds with zeros are called *no-load* funds. Sometimes a fund that does not charge an *up-front load* will make investors pay when they sell their fund shares. That figure is under the column with the heading "Exit." When you are charged at the time you sell your shares, it's called a *back-end load*. The funds that charge back-end loads sometimes have a small *r* after the fund name.

Just as for stock tables, newspapers usually include a chart that reminds you what the mutual fund table columns mean. Each paper does its own version, but they all guide you in the same way.

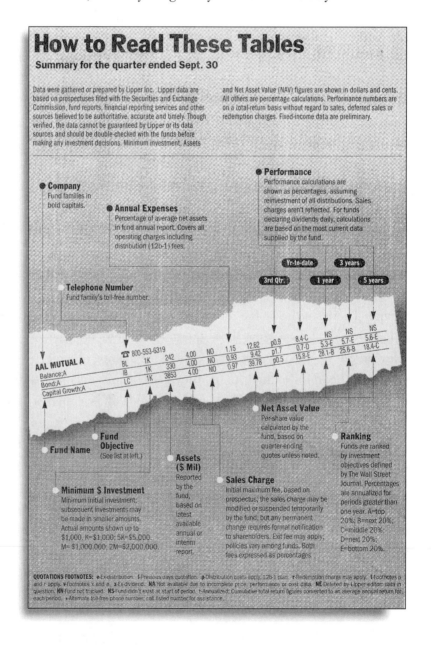

How to Read These Tables
Summary for the quarter ended Sept. 30

Data were gathered or prepared by Lipper Inc.. Lipper data are based on prospectuses filed with the Securities and Exchange Commission, fund reports, financial reporting services and other sources believed to be authoritative, accurate and timely. Though verified, the data cannot be guaranteed by Lipper or its data sources and should be double-checked with the funds before making any investment decisions. Minimum investment, Assets and Net Asset Value (NAV) figures are shown in dollars and cents. All others are percentage calculations. Performance numbers are on a total-return basis without regard to sales, deferred sales or redemption charges. Fixed-income data are preliminary.

Company
Fund families in bold capitals.

Annual Expenses
Percentage of average net assets in fund annual report. Covers all operating charges including distribution (12b-1) fees.

Performance
Performance calculations are shown as percentages, assuming reinvestment of all distributions. Sales charges aren't reflected. For funds declaring dividends daily, calculations are based on the most current data supplied by the fund.

Telephone Number
Fund family's toll-free number.

					3rd Qtr.	Yr-to-date	1 year	3 years	5 years
☎ 800-553-6319								8.4-C	NS	NS	NS
BL	1K	242	4.00	NO	1.15	12.62	p0.9	0.7-D	5.3-E	5.7-E	5.6-E
IB	1K	330	4.00	NO	0.93	9.42	p1.7	15.8-E	28.1-B	25.6-B	18.4-C
LC	1K	3853	4.00	NO	0.97	39.78	p0.5				

AAL MUTUAL A
Balance;A
Bond;A
Capital Growth;A

Net Asset Value
Per-share value calculated by the fund, based on quarter-ending quotes unless noted.

Ranking
Funds are ranked by investment objectives defined by The Wall Street Journal. Percentages are annualized for periods greater than one year. A=top 20%; B=next 20%; C=middle 20%; D=next 20%; E=bottom 20%.

Fund Name

Fund Objective
(See list at left.)

Assets ($ Mil)
Reported by the fund, based on latest available annual or interim report.

Minimum $ Investment
Minimum initial investment; subsequent investments may be made in smaller amounts. Actual amounts shown up to $1,000. K=$1,000; 5K=$5,000. M=$1,000,000; 2M=$2,000,000.

Sales Charge
Initial maximum fee, based on prospectus; the sales charge may be modified or suspended temporarily by the fund, but any permanent change requires formal notification to shareholders. Exit fee may apply; policies vary among funds. Both fees expressed as percentages.

QUOTATIONS FOOTNOTES: **e-** Ex-distribution. **t-** Previous day's quotation. **p-** Distribution costs apply, 12b-1 plan. **r-** Redemption charge may apply. **t-** Footnotes p and r apply. **v-** Footnotes x and e. **x-** Ex-dividend. **NA-** Not available due to incomplete price, performance or cost data. **NE-** Deleted by Lipper editor; data in question. **NN-** Fund not tracked. **NS-** Fund didn't exist at start of period. **t-** Annualized; Cumulative total return figures converted to an average annual return for each period. **z-** Alternate toll-free phone number; call listed number for assistance.

OK, that's it. As you can see, checking mutual fund tables is not so terribly different from looking at stock histories. It's actually a little bit easier, since you have the report card rankings to give you a quick clue. Now it's time to put what you've learned to work.

VANGUARD FDS		800-662-7447									
Intmdt-Tm Treas	IG	50K	1333	NO	NO	0.15	10.21	3.1	8.1	7.2A	6.0A	6.2A
Long-Tm Treas	LU	50K	442	NO	NO	0.15	10.62	2.8	11.8	9.5A	7.1A	7.1A
Sh Tm Treas	SU	50K	1048	NO	NO	0.15	9.97	2.5	5.7	6.1A	5.6A	5.8B
Asset Alloc	MP	3K	9045	NO	NO	0.49	24.79	1.1	6.2	11.4C	13.8A	17.0A
CA Ins Int Tx-Ex	IM	3K	1599	NO	NO	0.17	10.77	2.5	7.5	7.0A	5.0A	5.8A
CA Ins Lg Tx-Ex	NM	3K	1660	NO	NO	0.18	11.26	3.1	9.7	8.6A	5.2A	6.5A
Cap Oppty	XG	3K	5984	NO	NO	0.75	31.52	r0.8	31.2	80.6A	43.9A	28.3B
Convertible	MP	3K	373	NO	NO	0.55	14.98	2.5	14.4	37.9A	13.8A	15.1B
Energy	NR	3K	1243	NO	NO	0.48	28.41	r8.5	29.8	27.3C	5.0B	16.0B
Equity Income	EI	3K	2395	NO	NO	0.41	24.06	7.4	5.8	6.3D	9.4B	15.8A
Explorer Fund	SG	3K	4807	NO	NO	0.74	80.04	1.7	16.6	51.6C	16.1D	17.2C
FL Ins L-T Tx-Ex	NM	3K	888	NO	NO	0.18	10.94	2.3	7.3	7.0A	4.5A	5.9A
Glbl Ast All	MP	3K	112	NO	NO	0.58	11.02	r−0.3	2.9	7.7D	9.8C	10.8D
Glbl Equity	GL	3K	149	NO	NO	0.68	13.66	r−3.0	−3.4	6.8E	7.6D	11.0D
GNMA	MT	3K	13031	NO	NO	0.27	10.06	3.2	7.4	7.6A	5.9A	6.7A
Gold	AU	3K	321	NO	NO	0.77	6.98	r2.5	−16.8	−18.6A	−9.8A	−9.5A
Growth & Income	LV	3K	10146	NO	NO	0.37	35.71	1.6	−0.4	16.2A	16.5A	22.1A
Growth Equity	LG	10K	849	NO	NO	0.92	18.68	−1.2	8.2	51.1A	32.2A	30.4A
Health Care	HB	3K	15309	NO	NO	0.41	130.90	r9.5	46.0	59.7D	30.5B	30.6A
Hi Yld Corp	HC	3K	5630	NO	NO	0.29	7.04	r1.4	1.8	4.5A	4.2A	7.0A
Inflation-Protect Se	LU	3K	75	NO	NO	NA	10.15	2.1	NS	NS	NS	NS
Intl Gro	IL	3K	10144	NO	NO	0.58	20.79	−9.9	−7.6	12.6B	7.3C	10.7C
International Value	IL	3K	919	NO	NO	0.59	26.16	−9.6	−9.4	−2.6E	4.7D	7.4E
Intmdt Corp	IB	3K	1703	NO	NO	0.27	9.29	3.7	6.4	6.8A	5.2C	6.0B
Intmdt Treas	IG	3K	1639	NO	NO	0.27	10.44	3.2	8.1	7.1A	5.9A	6.1A
Lifestrategy Consv G	BL	3K	1794	NO	NO	NA	15.15	1.3	4.0	10.1C	10.0B	11.9C
Lifestrategy Growth	BL	3K	3740	NO	NO	NA	21.12	−0.5	0.2	13.1B	12.9A	16.1A
Lifestrategy Income	BL	3K	567	NO	NO	NA	13.04	2.4	6.3	8.6D	8.4C	9.7E
Star Moderate Gro	BL	3K	3818	NO	NO	NA	18.21	0.4	2.3	11.6C	11.5B	14.0B
Lg-Tm Corp	AB	3K	3611	NO	NO	0.30	8.19	3.4	6.5	5.6C	4.5C	6.0B
Lg-Tm Treas	LU	3K	1213	NO	NO	0.27	10.32	2.7	11.7	9.4A	6.9A	7.0A
MA Tax-Ex	SS	3K	162	NO	NO	0.20	9.47	2.7	7.8	6.7A	NS	NS
Morgan Growth	XG	3K	6187	NO	NO	0.43	22.55	−1.7	1.4	24.8E	18.4D	22.3D
Muni High Yield Tx-E	GM	3K	3007	NO	NO	0.18	10.27	2.7	6.8	5.4B	4.1A	5.6A
Muni Ins Lg-Tm Tx-Ex	NM	3K	2295	NO	NO	0.19	12.04	2.3	7.7	7.0A	4.5A	5.7A
Muni Intmdt-Tm Tx-Ex	IM	3K	8450	NO	NO	0.18	12.99	2.1	5.6	5.6A	4.3A	5.0B
Muni Long-Tm Tx-Ex	GM	3K	1628	NO	NO	0.18	10.64	2.3	7.5	6.7A	4.2A	5.7A
Muni Limited-Tm Tx-E	SM	3K	2754	NO	NO	0.18	10.62	1.7	4.1	4.4A	4.0A	4.3A
Muni Short-Tm Tx-Ex	SM	3K	1980	NO	NO	0.18	15.49	1.2	3.3	4.0B	3.8B	3.9C
NJ Ins L-T Tx-Ex	SS	3K	1197	NO	NO	0.19	11.40	2.5	7.2	6.5A	4.5A	5.5A
NY Ins L-T Tx-Ex	NM	3K	1590	NO	NO	0.20	10.68	2.3	8.0	7.1A	4.5A	5.6A
OH Ins L-T Tx-Ex	SS	3K	396	NO	NO	0.19	11.38	2.2	7.1	6.5A	4.3A	5.5A
PA Ins L-T Tx-Ex	SS	3K	1893	NO	NO	0.19	10.83	2.1	7.1	6.5A	4.4A	5.5A
Preferred Stk	MP	3K	209	NO	NO	0.36	8.75	2.8	1.5	−2.2E	1.8E	5.2E
Primecap	XC	3K	25071	NO	NO	0.51	68.75	−3.5	12.2	34.5A	23.4A	26.3A
REIT Index	SE	3K	1026	NO	NO	0.33	11.45	r7.5	21.8	20.9C	−0.3D	NS
Select Value	MV	3K	153	NO	NO	0.73	11.04	10.9	11.1	11.5E	−3.8E	NS
Star	BL	1K	8093	NO	NO	NA	18.51	5.1	9.0	15.0B	10.0B	14.0B
Sht-Tm Corp	SB	3K	7014	NO	NO	0.27	10.57	2.8	5.5	6.6A	5.7A	6.0A
Sht-Tm Federal	SU	3K	1447	NO	NO	0.27	9.99	2.5	5.6	6.3A	5.5A	5.8A
Strategic Equity	MV	3K	747	NO	NO	0.46	17.97	r4.9	7.2	23.2C	6.6C	16.0B
Sht-Tm Treas	SU	3K	1169	NO	NO	0.27	10.10	2.3	5.5	5.9B	5.5B	5.6B
Tax Mgd Balanced	BL	10K	416	NO	NO	0.20	19.29	r0.6	4.0	15.5A	12.1A	13.5B
Tx Mgd Cap App	XG	10K	3045	NO	NO	0.19	35.03	r−0.5	2.5	25.8E	19.8D	22.6D
Tx Mgd G&I	LC	10K	2577	NO	NO	0.19	31.17	r−0.9	−1.4	13.4D	16.5C	21.7B
Tx Mgd Intl	IL	10K	197	NO	NO	NA	10.54	r−8.0	−11.9	3.4D	NS	NS
Tx Mgd SmCp	SC	10K	324	NO	NO	0.19	14.21	r4.8	12.7	26.8C	NS	NS
US Growth	LG	3K	22331	NO	NO	0.39	46.33	1.1	6.4	27.9C	23.8C	25.3B
US Value	XV	3K	60	NO	NO	NA	10.84	10.3	NS	NS	NS	NS
Utilities	UT	3K	864	NO	NO	0.40	16.04	13.6	17.5	18.0D	16.3D	14.7E
Wellesley Income	MP	3K	6202	NO	NO	0.31	19.76	6.9	9.3	8.3D	7.2D	10.4D
Wellington Income	BL	3K	22423	NO	NO	0.30	28.12	4.7	3.4	6.0D	7.6D	12.9C
Windsor	XV	3K	15918	NO	NO	0.28	16.07	7.8	6.8	13.2B	5.1D	13.1C
Windsor II	LV	3K	23606	NO	NO	0.37	27.11	10.5	9.8	7.8D	7.8D	16.0D

Read the Mutual Fund Tables

Look on the Vanguard Funds listings in the table on the previous page and find a fund that ranks in the *A* category. Then find a fund than ranks in the *E* category. Has either improved or declined in performance over time? Now see if you can find the funds that are classified as growth funds and those that are growth-and-income funds. Next, pick one of the funds in the chart. Fill in the middle row of boxes in the table below. Next, look it up in a current newspaper or on-line. Fill in the bottom row of boxes. Has it improved or declined in performance over time?

	Fund Name	Fund Obj	One Year	Ranking Guide	Three Year	Ranking Guide
August 2000						
Today's Date						

	Fund Name (continued)	Five Year	Ranking Guide	Ten Year (if available)	Ranking Guide	Max Initial Charge
August 2000						
Today's Date						

What are the key things you looked at to determine the fund's history? Place an x next to each category that helped you.

FundName _____

FundObj _____

One Year Return _____

Three Year Return _____

Five Year Return _____

Ten Year Return _____

Max Sales Chrg _____

Billy Ray Picks Some Funds

Billy Ray decided he wanted to divide his savings into thirds, each with a different risk level. He did some research about investments, but he wasn't quite sure what mix would be best.

Billy Ray went to school with a young woman whose father was a financial planner, so he went to him, told him his plan, and asked for advice. He thought about all the things his friend's dad told him and looked over all the information he gave him. Then Billy Ray made his decision.

At age 20 Billy Ray bought three mutual funds. For his high-risk fund he picked the Alliance Technology Fund, Class B, which is managed by the Alliance Capital Group. For his medium-risk fund he chose the MFS Emerging Growth Fund, managed by MFS Investment Management. For his low-risk investment he bought shares in the Washington Mutual Investors Fund, managed by the American Funds Group. Each of these funds has a management style that fit his goals. Also, the Washington Mutual Investors Fund has no alcohol or tobacco stocks in it, and this appealed to him. He has stayed with these funds ever since. In his words, "I'm in for the duration." He adds to these three funds when he can, and he sits back and lets them earn money for him. But Billy Ray didn't stop here.

In this chapter you learned all about how to read the clues to pick your investments wisely. You learned:

- where stock tables are published
- how to understand the stock table abbreviations
- how to interpret stock table numbers
- where mutual fund tables are published
- how to understand mutual fund table abbreviations
- how to interpret mutual fund numbers

You now know the basic information needed to look at stock and mutual fund tables. You have all the tools in place to play the investment game. At this moment, you understand enough to walk into a brokerage office and place an order for stocks, bonds, or mutual funds, or you could do this over the phone or on-line. Yet with investments, just like sports, there are some big-picture issues you need to know before you become a highly skilled player. You need to learn some of the signs that tell you if the stock market is getting tired, or if workers are spending more than they did two years ago, and you need to know how and why the U.S. government tries to fix things. All of these issues have to do with the bigger economic picture, which is covered in the next chapter.

All About the Economy

WHY NIKES COST MORE WHEN IT FLOODS IN CHINA

Economics

TO MANY PEOPLE, especially adults, *economy* and *economics* are scary words. They're scary because adults hear these words a lot on the news and they might not always know what they really mean. These words don't have to be scary. They're very simple, especially when the economy is broken down into its various parts.

A famous economist named Alfred Marshall once said that *economics* is "the study of mankind in the ordinary business of life." That's really what it is. It's the study of life with a special interest in saving and spending. It's the study of money and how it circulates. It's the study of people and their saving patterns. It's the study of investing trends. It's the study of how people's minds work, and what makes them save or not save.

Economists study why people buy certain stocks or bonds, and then what causes them to sell them. And they study what things cost—both yesterday and today, and what they might cost tomorrow. The best part of all this is that you already know a lot about most of these things by now, so at the very least you need not be afraid.

Macroeconomics and Microeconomics

Before we get started, there are a couple of new terms you should know. These are *macroeconomics* and *microeconomics*. They are both big and pretty impressive words, and each feels good in your mouth when you say it. Think of Big Macs when you say macroeconomics because, in a way, the subject matter is like a Big Mac—it has it all. Macroeconomists know how many people work in the whole country and how many can't find jobs. They even know how many work in your state and how many are jobless in your town. They look at how many houses are built each month, and find out how many are built in California, Illinois, or Florida. They even look at weather patterns and know when it floods in China. They know how the floods in China cause your Nikes to cost more, because your Nikes are made in China. Macroeconomists study big things. The study of the details is left to microeconomists.

Microeconomics is not about the big picture; it's about all the little pieces that make up the big picture. It's about companies that make things and stores that sell things. It's about how companies that make similar products compare with each other, such as Nike and Reebok, or The Gap and Eddie Bauer, or Coca-Cola and Pepsi. It's about yearly sales for each of these companies, and how much they spend on television ads during the Super Bowl, and how much they earned per share of stock. Finally, it's about whether a particular company does better or worse than the other companies that sell the same products.

To sum up, macroeconomics is like seeing your city or town from one of those blimps that you see floating over ballparks and football stadiums. From this view you can see the bigger shapes of things like highways, schools, and churches. You can count the number of schools by the number of playgrounds or playing fields you see, or the number of churches by counting the number of steeples. But you can't see any details. You can't even find your own house. In contrast, microeconomics is like moving through your city or town on skates. You can skate past your school or a church, and then over to the shopping mall nearest your house. You can see that there are a lot of cars in the parking lot and you can even count the number of people going into The Gap. But you can't tell how many people are in Eddie Bauer in the mall on the other side of town unless you roller blade over there and count. Only when you compare the two stores can you tell which one is more successful.

$ Follow the Weather

Listen to the national news on television or on the radio. If you have cable, turn on the Weather Channel, or if you have access to the Internet, go to www.weather.com. See if there is a mention of a major weather event like a thunderstorm, snowstorm, tornado, or flood. Then, see if the news programs talk about businesses being closed or people unable to work because of the weather. Think about what these events have to do with the economy. If a lot of households are damaged, who will pay for the repairs? Will homeowners have to take money from their savings accounts? Who will rebuild the homes? Will local carpenters and electricians have more work than they can handle? Will they have to hire more workers?

Next listen to your local news or read your local newspaper. Find a news story that shows people affected by the weather. Have basements flooded? Have cars been stalled in deep water somewhere? Think about what that might mean for the economy of your town. Will your neighbors have to buy a new couch or easy chair? Will they buy the furniture from the store in town? Will the storeowner then have a lot more money to buy more furniture for his store?

The Economic Checkup

Let's start with the big picture, the macroeconomic picture. Remember that economics is about life. It's about jobs, savings, investing, and money. It's also about floods, hurricanes, tornados, and the damage they cause, and it's about who pays for the damage. Macroeconomists measure the economic health of our country. They're like family doctors. They decide if the country is sick, and then they decide on a cure.

How do economists measure our country's economic health? They do it just as your doctor does at your annual checkup. Your doctor weighs you, she feels your pulse, listens to your chest, looks in your ears, and makes you say "Ahh" when she puts that awful tongue depressor way back in your mouth. By checking all of these things, she can tell if you are healthy and growing at the proper rate. The only difference between a physical checkup by a doctor and an economic checkup by economists is that they check a different set of things. Here are the major questions economists ask when they check America's economic health:

- How many Americans want to work but can't find jobs?

- How many new houses are being started each month?

- How many back orders do factories have? (Here they're interested in factories that manufacture big-ticket items such as machinery, tractors, or cars.)

- How many new orders are being placed at factories that make consumer goods such as shoes, clothes, videos, and CDs?

- How much money is in circulation? Remember that money circulates from person to person as people buy and sell things and pay bills. Economists look at this circle for every consumer in the country.

The economy is like a giant jigsaw puzzle, and the answer to each of the checkup questions is a puzzle piece. As economists pick up one piece after another and fit it into place, the picture gets clearer. Finally, when enough pieces have been filled in, the picture comes together. By looking at each piece in connection to the others, economists can tell if the economy is healthy or sick. They also can do something about it if they see an economic cold coming on.

Economic Clues

Here are the clues economists get from key economy puzzle pieces:

Jobless claims This shows how many people are out of work. The official phrase is *unemployment figures*. If unemployment figures go down, it means that more people are working. When people work, they spend the money they make. If more people are working then there is more money in circulation and the economy grows.

Housing starts Housing starts give economists another clue about economic health. When people buy new houses, it means they feel good about their jobs and the amount of money they have to spend. It also means that the economy is strong and there is more money in circulation. If housing starts are down, it means just the opposite. It means that people are not so confident about their jobs, and they don't want to spend their money, especially on something as expensive as a house.

Durable goods Economists check on back orders for big manufactured products, like cars, planes, and tractors. These large, heavy products that last a long time are called *durable goods*. Economists check to see how many orders have been placed for durable goods, and then they count how many orders have not been filled. The ones that are not filled are called *back orders*. The number of back orders gives economists a clue about how confident companies are about their sales. For instance, if a lot of people want to buy cars, car dealers will place such big orders that car manufacturers can't keep up with them. That's a good sign for the economy.

New factory orders Economists also check new factory orders for consumer goods. *Consumer goods* are things that we use up, like shoes, cereal, and milk. Consumer goods have to be replaced fairly often, since we grow out of our shoes, and eat up all our cereal, and even if we don't drink all the milk, it goes sour and has to be thrown out. When people buy a lot of consumer goods, it means two things. First, it means there's a lot of money in circulation. Second, it means people feel good about the economy.

Leading economic indicators There's a quick way to do an economic check-up, just as a blood test can check for a lot of things at once. It's called the *Index of Leading Economic Indicators*, often shortened to leading indicators or the Index. The leading indicators make up a kind of monthly economic report card. Ten indicators, including the checkup questions we've already looked at, make up the Index. Each indicator is assigned a point value or grade depending on its strength of activity. When the points are all added up, the economy gets a score for the month. Economists learn a lot about America's economic growth based on whether the leading indicator score goes up or down from month to month. When it goes up three months in a row, it's a sign that the economy is growing. If it goes down three months in a row, economists start to worry that the economy is getting sick. Investors can tell the same things.

$ Check the Health of the Economy

Look in the business section of a newspaper for graphs or discussions of the four indicators discussed above: jobless claims, housing starts, durable goods, and new factory orders. Are housing starts going up or down? What does that mean? Now look at the other indicators. What are the most recent unemployment figures? When thinking of all these indicators together, how would you say the economy is doing?

Now look for a leading indicators graph. Are the indicators going up or down? What does that mean for investors? Sit down and talk to someone about your views. Explain why you think the economy is healthy or getting sick. You may even decide to use what you've learned for a class report. If you can say it, it means you know it.

The Health of the Economy and the Doctor: The Federal Reserve System

One of the best ways to measure the economic health of the country is to measure the money supply. *Money supply* means the cash people have at their fingertips to spend on things. It's measured by the amount of money families have in bank accounts and the investments they have in funds that can be sold immediately. The leading indicators that were discussed above provide a pretty clear picture of the economy puzzle. When economists discover the money supply piece, the jigsaw puzzle is complete.

There is something very special about the money supply. Not only does the money supply help economists measure the country's economic health, it can also be used as medicine if the economy shows signs of getting sick. A special group of economists does this. They work for the Federal Reserve System and serve on the Federal Reserve Board, which is usually referred to as "the Fed." The Fed can regulate the money supply, which makes it very powerful. In fact, economists and investors eagerly watch the Fed's every move.

In many families, one person is in charge of paying bills and balancing the checkbook. In the United States it's the same way, but instead of one person, our country has a group of seven people who keep track of the nation's checkbook. The Fed members are appointed by the president of the United States and, if approved by Congress, they serve a 14-year term. This means they become very familiar with the health of the economy, just as your family doctor is very familiar with you.

The seven Fed members, along with a special committee called the Open Market Committee, are the people who keep a constant watch on the money supply in our country. They are the doctors who dole out the medicine to keep the economy healthy.

A Giant Allowance

The money supply is like a giant allowance, and the country does exactly what you do with your allowance. It spends most and sometimes saves some. The key is this: if people in America have more money to spend, they spend it. If they have less, they don't spend it. By controlling the money supply, the Fed controls how much Americans spend. (I'll explain how they do this next.) It all has to do with the amount of money in circulation.

Remember that the Fed economists carefully watch the leading indicators. By doing these regular economic checkups, the Fed can tell if the economy is getting a little hyperactive or if it's getting slow and sluggish. They call the hyperactivity *inflation*. When the economy is suffering from inflation, prices go up. This is because people have more cash to spend. Remember that when a lot of people want to buy the same stock, the seller can charge more? Well, it's the same with most everything we buy. Say your mom or dad gets a raise in September and your family has more money to spend for the holidays than usual. But a lot of other people received raises, too. Everyone feels confident so they all decide to buy more holiday gifts, including Sony's newest electronic game. Sony knows it's going to be a big seller, and it figures people will pay a lot to get one. So Sony puts a higher price on the game; in other words, Sony inflates the price.

If the price of one product goes up, that's OK, but if the prices of food, gasoline, and clothing all go up at once, that's bad news. It means that the value of a dollar has gone down, because you can't buy as much as you used to. If inflation gets out of hand the economy doesn't work as well as it should, so the Fed keeps a close eye on prices.

A sluggish economy is the opposite of an inflationary economy. When the economy is sluggish, economists are afraid it might go into what they call a *recession*. A recession means the economy is incredibly sluggish, hardly able to move. The Fed tries to take action before a sluggish economy goes into a recession.

Economists diagnose a sluggish economy when spending is down. They can see this by looking at some of the indicators. When a lot of people are unemployed, housing starts are down, and there aren't many back orders for cars and trucks people feel poor. The Fed keeps its finger on the country's emotional pulse as well as its financial pulse.

Consumer Confidence—Even the Country Can Have an Attitude

The economy has moods, or at least shoppers have moods. When we're in a good mood, we tend to do things like go out to movies and get hot fudge sundaes on the way home. We may even stop at a bookstore and buy a couple of new books. When we're in a good mood we tend to spend money, but when we're in a bad mood we don't like to go out at all. We stay home and mope, and we tend to hang on to every penny. Economists have a term for our moods. It's called *consumer confidence. Consumer* is another word for someone who buys things. Since all of us buy things, even if it's only a red licorice stick, we are all consumers. High consumer confidence means that we feel good about our current and future money supply, like when it's early summer and you know you'll have a lot of yard jobs before it gets cold. Low consumer confidence means just the opposite.

Economists spend a lot of time tracking consumer confidence for a couple of reasons. Consumer confidence reflects the health of the economy—its strength or weakness. At the same time, consumer confidence can change the health of the economy. Let's say that the economy is healthy; that is, unemployment is low and people are buying cars. But consumers don't feel good about the future. Some of them are afraid the plant where they work is going to close, others are upset because houses cost more than they can afford. So they mope around—they don't go out and they don't spend much money. When a lot of consumers start to mope around, the economy starts to mope around, too. It gets sluggish. Sometimes the Fed even has to step in and put us on an easy-money diet (explained on page 83) so that the economy won't get really sick.

Consumer confidence can help heal the economy, too. Let's say this time that the economy is sluggish for several months, but it's been a good growing season for farmers because there was a lot of rain after their crops were planted. Also, two new car plants are being built in North Carolina that will provide hundreds of new jobs. Americans are happy and employed, so they're not afraid of the future. Because they're not afraid, they begin to spend some money. As consumer money begins to flow back into the economy, the economy starts to speed up and before long, it's healthy again.

These patterns are called *economic cycles*. The word *cycle* comes from a Greek word that means circle or wheel. The economy goes round and round, and consumer confidence does the same thing. Sometimes it's low, then it gets high, and then it gets low again; and sometimes consumer confidence drives the economic wheel.

Check Inflation

Do an inflation check. Try to remember how much you or your folks paid for new school shoes or a winter coat last year. If you can't remember, ask someone in your family who might remember. Then go to the mall and check the prices for the same shoes and winter coat. Did the prices stay the same, or do they cost more this year? You might check other things you bought last year, such as CDs, video games, or the cost to rent a video.

Ask an adult about gasoline prices. Is gas more or less expensive this year than last year? What about food prices? If you don't usually help with the shopping, ask an adult who does. What about the price of milk, cereal, and peanut butter? Copy the table below to keep track of your comparisons. When you compare the figures, you will get a clear idea of whether or not we're in a period of inflation.

Inflation Check		
	This Year's Price	*Last Year's Price*
Shoes		
Winter Coat		
Logo Sweatshirt		
CD		
Video Game		
Big Mac		
Milk		
Cereal		
Gasoline		
Anything Else You Want to Compare		

If you want to get fancy, you can express the inflation increase or decrease as a percentage. If prices have gone up, subtract last year's price from this year's, and then divide last year's price into the difference. Move the decimal point two places to the right. The number you get is the percentage increase in inflation for one year. For example, if sweatshirts sold for $18 last year but for $20 this year, the inflation increase is 11% (20 − 18 = 2; 2 ÷ 18 = .11 or 11%). If prices have gone down, subtract this year's price from last year's price, and then divide last year's price into the difference. Move the decimal point two places to the right. The number you get is the percentage decrease in inflation for one year.

If you completed this part of the activity, then you just did what economists do every day. Congratulations!

Regulating the Money Supply

Based on the diagnosis of inflation or recession, the Fed will prescribe one of two things. It will either put us on a tough diet called a *tight-money policy* to help control inflation, or it will put us on a pretty good diet called an *easy-money policy* to help a sluggish economy avoid a recession. Another way to say it is that the Fed either decreases on increases the country's allowance.

When the Fed enacts a tight- or an easy-money policy, it is regulating the money supply. The Fed can regulate the money supply in a number of ways, but the most common way is for the Fed to buy or sell government securities. (Remember those Treasury notes and bonds from Chapter 3?) The Fed buys or sells treasuries the same way we make our trades in stocks or bonds. The only difference is that the Fed does it every day. Each morning, shortly after 11 o'clock, the New York Federal Reserve Bank either buys or sells treasury securities. If the Fed thinks there is too much money floating around out there, it can decide to take some of it back by selling treasuries. Banks or brokerage houses buy treasuries because they have customers who would like to invest in them. When banks buy them, it uses up some of their cash and they can't lend it to people for cars, homes, or college educations. Therefore, the money supply is tightened and economists say the Fed is following a tight-money policy. On the other hand, if the Fed thinks the economy is getting sluggish—people are not spending money—then it buys some treasuries. When the Fed buys treasuries from banks or brokerage houses, all that cash the Fed paid for them is put back into circulation, which makes it easier for people to borrow money from banks for cars and houses. When this happens we say the Fed is following an easy-money policy.

The other way that the Fed regulates the money supply is to change the discount rate. The *discount rate* is the interest rate the Fed charges local banks to borrow money from the Federal Reserve System. If the Fed decides the economy is growing too quickly and fears that prices will rise too high, it tries to slow it down. It makes banks pay more to borrow from the Fed. That is, it increases the discount rate. If the Fed thinks the economy is getting sluggish because consumer spending is down, it tries to pick it up. It charges banks a lower rate to borrow money; that is, it lowers the discount rate.

When the Fed acts to increase or decrease the discount rate, it's like hitting the first domino in a domino snake. When banks have to pay more to borrow money, they usually decide they don't want to borrow as much, or they may even decide not borrow any at all. This means that they have less money to lend out and are charging higher rates for the money they do loan, which cuts down the money supply. On the other hand, if the Fed charges banks less to borrow money, banks may decide to borrow as much as they can. This means there's more money circulating and it's easier to borrow. It's the allowance thing again. The Fed either decreases or increases the country's allowance.

The Fed is able to make money regulation policies because it runs America's national bank. I should really say banks, because there's not just one big bank called "the National Bank of America." There are 12 big banks. These 12 banks are called district banks, and they are spread all over the United States. Each part of the country has its own Fed-run bank. In addition to these 12 banks, there are 25 middle-sized banks called regional banks, also spread all over the country. The key thing to remember is that the banks that make up the Federal Reserve System are the biggest banks in the country, and when a smaller bank runs a little low on cash, it turns to a Fed bank for a loan.

The Fed Is More than a Doctor

The Fed does a lot more than regulate the nation's money supply. As I just mentioned, the Fed is in charge of the district and regional banks that make up America's national banking system. These are the banks that take old money out of circulation and issue new money, covered in Chapter 1.

The Fed also serves as a safe deposit box for foreign governments. Foreign countries store gold in the Federal Reserve Bank in New York City to use when money changes hands between countries. It is stored in a big vault that holds approximately 10,000 tons of gold. That's a lot of gold, and it's estimated to be the most gold kept in one place anywhere in the world.

As for the national checkbook, the Fed also keeps track of bank accounts for the U.S. Treasury and other government offices. It writes more than 80 million Treasury checks a year, including checks for your grandparents' retirement funds. Not only does it write the checks, it also has to keep a national check register. Can you imagine keeping track of 80 million checks? Not only do they keep track of balancing the checkbook, the Fed also makes sure that the banks in the Federal Reserve System are following all the rules that the government has set to protect their money.

As if the Fed didn't have enough to do, it also is the national clearinghouse for checks. What this means is that every time you write a check, or your parent receives a paycheck, or someone pays a bill, the Fed helps those checks get to the right bank—and quickly. That's every check written by everybody every day. That totals more than 15 billion checks a year—that's 15,000,000,000! As you can see, the Federal Reserve, with all of these essential responsibilities, is very important to this country's economy.

$ Visit a Federal Reserve Bank

Wherever you live, try to visit a Federal Reserve district or regional bank. The 12 district banks are located in Boston, New York, Philadelphia, Richmond (Virginia), Cleveland, Chicago, St. Louis, Minneapolis, Kansas City, Dallas, and San Francisco. If you live in New York City or anywhere nearby, visit the gold vaults in the New York Federal Reserve Bank. They give guided tours, and you'll learn a lot.

You can find out the locations and tour information for the regional Fed banks by going to www.frb.org. From that site you can find everything you need to know about the Fed system and the individual banks. For example, the New York Federal Reserve Bank is located at 33 Liberty Street, New York, NY 10045 and the phone number is (212) 720-6130.

$ Find the Fed in the Media

Because the Fed is so central to this country's economy, you'll often hear the words "Federal Reserve Board" or "the Fed" on television and radio news programs, or you may read these words in the newspaper. See if you can find the Federal Reserve Board mentioned in the business section. Count the number of times the Fed shows up. Now turn on a television news program and listen to the business portion of the broadcast. Is the Fed mentioned? How many times? If you have cable television, turn on a business channel and count how many times the Fed is mentioned in one 15-minute period.

Billy Ray Is Confident About the Economy

In 1998 Billy Ray was 21, playing basketball for the Georgetown College Tigers. He was still a star, and still called "the Legend." His mowing business was going well, and he was putting his earnings into his mutual funds, but he was starting to think about investing his savings in another way. He wanted to buy some land.

He started looking around, and before long he found the parcel of land of his dreams—a 7.2-acre piece of farmland on the outskirts of Mount Sterling. The property had a pond on it, and he thought it would be great to build a house there some day. Billy Ray had a girlfriend and wanted to get married in a few years. But the farmland was more than a place to build a house; Billy Ray thought it would be a good investment.

Mount Sterling was growing, and the people moving into town were building houses on the outskirts of town. As more people want land, the land will increase in value, just as when a lot of people want to buy a stock that has a limited number of shares. Billy Ray was confident that Mount Sterling would continue to grow because there were new factories on the edge of town, major universities 35 miles away in three directions, and several small colleges nearby. He thought that before long those 7.2 acres would be worth a lot more than the asking price, so he decided to buy the parcel.

He went to the bank again, and instead of asking for a small business loan he applied for a mortgage. A *mortgage* is a type of loan that helps people buy a house or land. The bank makes the borrower pay part of the cost of the property and then lends him the money for the rest, with the understanding that he will pay the bank a certain interest rate to use its money for a specified period of time. Sometimes this time period can be as long as 30 years. (Remember from Chapter 2 that one way the bank can pay you interest on your savings account is by letting other people borrow your money.) Mortgages are one of the most popular kinds of loans, because hardly anyone has enough money to buy a house or land with his savings.

Because Billy Ray had been planning to look for land since the previous winter, he had enough savings set aside to put 10% down on the property; therefore his mortgage was for 90% of the cost of the land. Billy Ray being Billy Ray, he started immediately to pay more on his monthly mortgage than he had to. The sooner he could pay off his mortgage, the sooner he wouldn't have to pay the bank to use it's money, and before long he nearly had his mortgage paid off. Plus, his prediction was right— land was getting scarce around Mount Sterling, and his land had increased in value in just one year. So even as Billy Ray was paying down his mortgage, his land was already worth more than he paid for it.

The days were beginning to get shorter and winter was on the way— Billy Ray's thinking time. Billy Ray started thinking about ways to make the best use of his investment in land.

In this chapter you learned all about the economy. You learned about:
- the terms macroeconomics and microeconomics and how economists use each
- the major clues to America's economy puzzle
- the Federal Reserve system, its functions, and how central it is to this country's economy
- money supply
- the meaning and importance of consumer confidence

You deserve to feel proud of all that you now understand—it's more than many adults know about how our economy works. To celebrate, go into the kitchen, pour yourself a big bowl of your favorite cereal, add a sliced banana, and pour on the milk. Then, as you eat, read the cereal box to discover what company produced it. You've just picked up a couple of potential stock investment tips. You'll find more suggestions on how to gather these tips and information in the next chapter.

All About Stock Picking

WHAT YOUR TOOTHPASTE TELLS YOU

Picking Stocks

NOW IT'S TIME to put it all together. You know about money and about savings. You know about the miracle of compounding, and you know the difference between saving and investing. You know about Wall Street and about stock exchanges and about the Dow Jones Industrial Average. You know what to say when you want to place an order for a stock or a mutual fund. You know how to read stock tables and how to compare stocks to see which one is the best buy. You know about the economy and

89

the Fed and leading indicators and consumer confidence. You know everything you need to know to be an investor except for one thing: how to pick the right stock. That's what this chapter is all about. The tools for becoming a good stock picker are actually right at your fingertips.

Just Turn on the Lights

Stocks are divided into sectors just as music CDs are divided into categories. A stock's *sector* simply describes the type of company that is listed on a stock exchange. Instead of "rock" or "R&B" or "country-western," stocks are listed under categories like "transportation," "financial," or "utilities." The names sound pretty boring when you compare them to music categories, but it's not so boring when you start making money from your utility or transportation investments.

One of the most popular stock sectors for the last century has been the utility sector. Utility companies provide us with gas for heating, electricity for lights and air conditioning, water for sprinkling the yard and flushing toilets, and telephone service. When your family comes home late at night, it may be Duke Energy (DUK) that provides the electricity when your Mom reaches around the corner and hits the kitchen light switch. (Note: throughout this chapter each company name is followed by its stock market abbreviation.) When it's your turn to do the dishes, it may be American Water Works (AWK) that makes the soap bubble way up when you turn the water on full force, or that fills the dishwasher if you're lucky enough to have one. Utility companies provide us with these essentials, now and in the future.

One place to start to learn about utility companies is in your own town. Ask an adult if you can look at the family's utility bills—the bills for water, electricity, gas, and telephone service. By looking at the bills you will see the name of the company that provides your home these services. If you live in the South Atlantic states, Duke Energy Corporation (DUK) may provide your power and BellSouth (BLS) your phone service. If you live near Washington, D.C., it may be the Washington Gas Light Company (WGL) that heats your furnace or provides you with gas to cook your food. No matter where you live in the United States, or even in the world, you might see AT&T Corporation (T) on a bill. It used to be the biggest phone company in the country, and it still provides phone service, but now it's more interested in wireless services like Internet transmission and cellular phones—two fast-growing markets.

All of the utility companies I've mentioned so far are considered good investments by a lot of people. That does not mean, though, that all utility companies are good buys. Utility companies are just like any other stock. You need to look into their history and their financial data before you make an investment decision. Chapter 8 lists books and on-line addresses that will help you learn more about individual stocks.

A lot of investors purchase utility stocks for income because utility companies usually pay steady dividends. My mother and stepfather owned shares in a number of electric and gas companies. They were retired and wanted that income coming in on a regular basis. Utilities are not just for older people, though. Utilities provide a stable base for anyone's investment portfolio. Since people will always need water, electricity, and telephones, they're good investments, even for kids.

Dividend Reinvestment Plans, or DRIPs, help make these utility stocks even better investments. DRIPs allow investors to reinvest their dividends rather than take the dividends in cash. This means that approximately four times a year you'll get to buy a little more stock. You sign up for the DRIP plan with the company that issues your stock. When you buy the stock to begin with, the company may ask if you want to take your dividends or reinvest them. If the company doesn't ask the question, you should. Just say, "Do you offer Dividend Reinvestment Plans?" If the person you are speaking to hesitates, say you are a beginning investor and that you would really rather own more stock than have the cash. If this kind of program is not already available, maybe you'll be able to talk the company into it.

Have You Looked at Your Toothpaste Lately?

Another interesting sector is called consumer staples. *Staples* are the products that we use every day. Because we use them every day, we use them up and have to buy more. This means that the companies that make staple products are usually good investments.

You already know a lot of companies in this sector, but you just haven't thought of them in terms of investment possibilities. These include Coca-Cola (KO), Colgate-Palmolive (CL), Gillette (G), Johnson & Johnson (JNJ), Procter & Gamble (PG) and Sara Lee (SLE). I don't need to tell you what Coca-Cola (KO) makes, and I don't need to point out that Coca-Cola is something some families buy over and over. You probably already know that the Colgate-Palmolive Company (CL) makes tooth-paste and toothbrushes. What you may not know is that Colgate-Palmolive also makes deodorant, bath and kitchen cleanser, laundry soap, and diet pills. A lot of companies in the consumer staples sector make more things than people think about. The Sara Lee Corporation (SLE) is a good example. If you've heard of Sara Lee, you probably know of it because of its sweet rolls and cookies. What you may not know is that Sara Lee also makes Ball Park Franks and sells coffee and tea, clothes, bug spray, and air fresheners. The thing to remember about stocks in the consumer staple sector is that they are usually pretty stable. Although the value of a share may go up and down a little bit, you are not likely to lose all of your investment. That's because of the type of products these companies make—when people use up one of these products, they usually buy more.

Search for Consumer Staples

Go on a consumer staple sector search. Look in the linen closet and under the bathroom sink of your home. List the names of the companies that make the things you use every day. Sometimes you have to really look to find the name of the company, but it's always there somewhere on the packaging. Be sure to check the toothpaste, bath soap, razor blades, toilet paper, and cotton swabs.

Now look in the kitchen. Make a list of the companies that make the things under the sink. Check the dishwashing soap, sink cleansers, and paper towels. Next check the cupboards where your family keeps food. Who makes the cereal, peanut butter, soup, and macaroni and cheese?

Finally, look in the financial section of the paper to see if you can find any of the company names on your list. Jot down the company letter symbol and pick three companies to keep track of for the next three months.

Product	Manufacturer Symbol	Stock Price	Current Price	Month 1 Price	Month 2 Price	Month 3 Price

Computer Stocks

Every time you turn on the computer at home or in the classroom, you are touching a potential stock purchase. It may be the computer itself, made by Compaq Computer (CPQ), Dell Computer Corporation (DELL), or International Business Machines Corporation (IBM); or it might be the software that runs the computer, like Microsoft Corporation (MSFT) or Intel Corporation (INTC).

The stocks of companies that supply equipment for computers and other electronic devices are called technology stocks or just technologies. Technologies are big right now. (I probably didn't need to tell you that.) You may even be in class with someone who just designed a new software system to make it easier to buy boomerangs from Australia on-line.

Buying a technology stock is a lot different than buying a utility or a consumer staple stock. While the process is the same, the end result may be different because stocks of technology companies are riskier investments than stocks of utilities or consumer staples companies. This doesn't mean you shouldn't buy them. It just means you're taking a bigger chance with some technology stocks than you would with some other stock companies. Remember the investment formula: the higher the risk, the greater the potential return. So, if your technology company turned out to be a good bet, you could make a lot more money than you would with a phone or cereal company.

Not all technology companies are high risk. The ones that I named already like IBM (IBM) and Intel (INTC) are pretty safe. There are others, such as Lucent Technologies (LU), that provide the world with telecommunications equipment, and they are probably as safe as MacDonald's Corporation (MCD).

The Key

The key to all this stuff about stock picking is to simply look around you, then think, "What does my family buy over and over, and who makes it?" My grandchildren and I sometimes sit around the dinner table talking about how to chose a stock. When we do this, someone is always jumping up and checking who makes our favorite foods. One of my granddaughters eats a lot of macaroni and cheese, and I mean *a lot*. She should definitely invest in the stock of her favorite brand.

Another thing to think about is who makes your favorite clothes. That's something else my grandchildren do—check their own labels and poll their friends about their favorite clothes and who makes them. If you do this, it's best to write it all down.

Films are another area to check. You already know about Disney (DIS). What other companies produce films that people stand in long lines to see, or that run for week after week after week? What film producers or directors keep winning Academy Awards? Don't forget about music. Who produces the CDs you buy? Is there one company that shows up all the time? Check with friends, too, to find out who they listen to and what label this music is on. Asking people what they think of a particular store, music company, or soap product is a great way to collect information. When you ask these kinds of questions, you're doing a "consumer satisfaction survey." Companies pay a lot of money to marketing specialists for this kind of information. You can do your own survey just by looking around and asking people questions. Collecting this information will help inform your stock choices.

Don't forget to think about shopping, too. Wal-Mart (WMT) is big right now. The stores are always full, the service is good, the lines are short, and you can return things without a hassle. Watch for those kind of things whenever you shop.

Ask the adults in your family if they've ever shopped at Ethan Allen (ETH) for furniture or seen one of its catalogues. What about Bed, Bath & Beyond (BBBY)? Get an adult's opinion about the quality of the things these stores sell and whether these stores or others might be good investments. Oh, and don't forget Home Depot (HD). Home Depot is always jammed with people buying lumber, windows, light switches, and kitchen cabinets.

Everywhere you look, if you really think about it, you will see a potential stock purchase. Then do your stock analysis homework and, if it looks like a good bet, jump in.

Remember, not all of your stock purchases will be winners. If more than half are, you've truly learned about investing. In fact, even when you lose money on a stock or a mutual fund, you learn things. My grandfather used to say to me, "If you walk down the street with a fool and don't learn something, it might not be the fool's fault." It's true. You learn just as much from the choices that don't turn out well as from the ones that do.

Conduct a Consumer Survey

Make a list of some of your favorite things, like clothes, musicians, and movies. You can also include some of your parents' favorite things, and the stores where they like to shop. Write down the labels or brands on the objects you've listed. Keep track of the number of times you see someone wearing clothes on your brand list. The chart below will make it easy.

	FAVORITE THINGS	NUMBER OF TIMES YOU SPOTTED THIS ITEM
Music:		
Food:		
Shoes:		
Clothing:		
Video Game:		

What do your results tell you about the popularity of your choices? See if you can find the stock symbols for these companies. Does the stock for any of these companies look like a good investment opportunity? Use what you learned in Chapter 5 to make your decision.

Don't Forget About Mutual Funds

Stock mutual funds give you a way to buy shares in a number of stocks at one time and for less money than buying all those shares separately. (Refer to Chapter 3 for the differences in buying shares of a stock and buying shares of a mutual fund.) Mutual funds come in all shapes and sizes. There are thousands to choose from. How do you pick the right ones?

Remember that Billy Ray decided that he wanted to split his investments into three parts—one-third for high-risk investments, one-third for medium risk, and one-third for low risk. That's one way to pick funds, and it's a very good way.

Mutual funds make it easy for you to think in terms of risk because they are classified by investment goals, which give you some good clues about risk levels. Instead of thinking in terms of sectors, like utilities or consumer staples, you make choices between goals like current income funds, growth funds, and growth and income funds. Under mutual fund investment goal headings there are even further subheadings that define the goal. These headings include terms like "balanced" or "equity income" under growth and income funds, or "aggressive growth," "small company growth," and "global equity" in the growth funds category. There are even sector funds that have only stocks of utility companies. Some have only technology stocks. The thing to remember is that these terms are descriptions that give the investor a general idea of the kinds of stocks in the funds.

Each of the investment goals relates to a certain level of risk. For example, Billy Ray's low-risk fund is an income fund in the Washington Mutual Investors Fund group of funds. The fund manager invests in stocks and bonds that give Billy Ray a steady return on his investment with little chance of losing his money.

Billy Ray's medium-risk fund is a growth and income fund called the MFS Emerging Growth Fund. Part of the fund is invested in stable securities that provide income, but there are also stocks that don't provide current income. Those stocks have a chance to increase in value and make money for the shareholders in the future.

Billy Ray's high-risk fund is a growth fund, Alliance Technology Fund, Class B, that invests in technology companies. Some are small companies that are just starting up, and others are more established. With high-risk funds you take a chance of your fund losing value some years. You may even lose money on the fund if the portfolio managers gambled on some companies that just couldn't make it. But you also have the chance of increasing your investment like crazy, and it can feel really good to take that chance.

Check into Fund Families

Another way to pick mutual funds to fit your investment goal is to use a family of funds. Remember that a *family of funds* is a cozy way of saying that one mutual fund investment company has a lot of fund types available. It's just like the Kellogg Company makes cereal, but it doesn't just make one type. It makes Corn Flakes, Cheerios, Shredded Wheat, Rice Krispies, and granola. Mutual fund families are the same. An investor says to herself, "I invested in Oak Associates White Oak Growth Stock Fund and it did well. I think I'll see if Oak Associates has an aggressive growth fund." It does—the Pine Oak Aggressive Stock Fund.

Mutual fund families make it easy for you. They send you information that shows each of the funds they manage, and the goal of each fund. They will even include the names of some of the stocks each fund invests in.

Find Fund Families

Look in the business section of the newspaper under mutual funds. Look for fund company names. They are often in bold type. Now look for the companies that have the most funds listed under them. See if you can tell which companies offer the most fund choices to investors.

After you've found a large family of funds, look under the heading marked "YTD % Ret" (Year to Date % Return). Compare the different returns. Look at the names of the funds. Can you tell anything about the type of stocks that are in the fund from the names? See if you can determine any connection between the names of the funds and the YTD % Return. Now ask yourself, "If I were going to split my investment into three risk levels as Billy Ray did, does this company have a fund for each investment goal?"

Investing in Stocks or Mutual Funds

Which is the best investment—shares of stock or shares of mutual funds? How about investing in both? Mutual funds spread your investments out over a number of stock companies. By buying shares in a stock mutual fund, you protect your investment from total loss. On the other hand, the portfolio managers who manage your mutual fund investments do not work for free. You have to pay them part of what you earn on your investment each year to make stock choices for you. This is definitely something to take into account when you choose your investments.

When you purchase shares of stock directly from a broker or on-line, you pay a one-time fee to the broker who bought your stock for you through one of the exchanges. (Remember how the broker writes a ticket?) After that initial fee, there are no more costs. You don't have to pay a management fee year after year. You can pay yourself and invest what you pay yourself in more stock.

So, the answer to the question of whether to invest in a mutual fund or stock is this: consider investing in both. You will sleep at night knowing that a portfolio manager is watching over the stocks in your mutual fund, and you will smile to yourself during the day when you see that a stock you picked on your own just gained 9% in value. That gain is because of something you thought might happen and did! Plus, there might be rumors of a merger where the stockholders will get two shares of the new company for each share in the old company. That's worth more than a smile; that's worth a laugh out loud and maybe a little dance step or two, especially since you know you figured it all out on your own.

Billy Ray Pays Himself

Billy Ray has a theory. It's that you pay yourself. Right off the top of any money he earns, he sets aside money to save and invest. He's done that since he was a kid shoveling snow in the winter or cutting grass in the summer. He says it's like paying bills. Instead of paying for clothes or other things you want to buy, you first pay yourself. This money you pay yourself goes into your savings. So Billy Ray is paying himself and continues to plan his investments.

In the winter of 1999, Billy Ray was 22 and playing basketball for the Georgetown Tigers when he began to think about assets and equity. He had money in his savings account and in his mutual funds. Those were his *assets*. He could continue to put money in his funds, which would increase his assets. But he wondered whether he should start to build up equity. He already had equity in his farmland. *Equity* is the difference between the value of land and the amount still owed on it. (Remember that Mt. Sterling is growing and land values have increased.) Plus, Billy

Ray had been paying extra money on his mortgage. So he spent some dark winter evenings trying to decide the best place to put his money.

By the end of winter, Billy Ray decided to go for equity. He decided to use the money he made from his mowing company the next year to bring water, gas, and electricity to his land. He also decided to build a big garage with a small kitchen and bathroom, which he could live in for a year or so until he got married. He already had

Photo courtesy of Billy Ray Fawns

Billy Ray

some equity in the land and a good record of making his mortgage payments. So he went back to the bank and asked to borrow some more money. He used the increased value of his farm to get a bigger mortgage, and then he got started. He put a road into the heart of the land. He built a water supply for a future house, plus a sewer system. Those two things cost the most. Then he brought in electricity so he could start to build his garage. He figured that after a couple of years his land would be worth even more, plus he had made all the improvements on his property, which further increased the value.

Billy Ray's goal was to build a large house on his land. He wanted to build up equity in the land and then go back to the bank to ask for a loan for the house. He hoped to have enough equity in his land in the future to get his mortgage without having to spend any of his savings.

Don't forget that all the time he was building equity, his mutual funds were still earning money for him and increasing his assets. Way to go, Billy Ray!

In this chapter you learned about picking stocks. You learned about:
- stock sectors and stock abbreviations
- dividend reinvestment plans
- consumer surveys
- choosing between stocks and mutual funds, or having some money in each

The next chapter will help you ask some good questions and find some good answers along the investment trail.

All About All of the Above

AND WHERE TO GO FOR MORE

Good Questions Usually Get Good Answers

WHEN I WAS a graduate student at the University of Michigan, I sometimes felt my brain couldn't hold all the facts that I was learning. After a few years of more and more facts, I thought that any day I might start to forget what I learned at the beginning of my college career. Then I realized something that I have never forgotten: the sign of what you know about a subject is not the number of facts you can hold in your head. When you really understand a subject, it means you know the important questions to ask and where to find the answers.

I've thought of that realization a lot since I began writing this book. You don't need to remember all the facts I've included; you just need to understand enough to ask good questions. You also need to know where to get the best answers. These two tools will pave the road to your successful investment future. Remember that Billy Ray was never afraid to ask questions.

This chapter lists some questions and then gives you the answers. A lot of the questions have to do with finding information. Where do I look for mutual fund information? What are the e-mail addresses for on-line brokers? Are there places to look for stock information on-line? Here we go!

How do I find out more information on saving and investing?
- The first place to start is the library. Start by looking under "investing," "economy," "stocks," "bonds," or "stock market."

- Another good resource is a bookstore that has a business section. You can find a book to answer almost any question you have. The people behind the information counter will usually show you exactly where to look, if you can't find a book on the topic yourself. You can also look for the business and personal finance magazine section. Then you can browse through these and see which ones you like best.

- Your computer is another resource. If you have an encyclopedia CD-ROM, you can search this for information using the terms listed above for library searches.

- If you can go on-line, there are dozens of sites to check. Your home page is a place to start. There are often lists of subjects in a sidebar to start a search. Just click on "business" or "investments."

- Many mutual fund investment companies provide information and training. You can either call them directly to see if they have information they can send you, or you can check their sites on-line. A company's on-line address is usually the same as its fund family name.

- Most daily newspapers have a business section that gives you up-to-the-minute information on economic data, stock closing prices, and news stories about different companies.

- Check out newspapers and news magazines that are just about business. These include: the *Wall Street Journal* (daily), *Barrons* (weekly), *Forbes* (weekly), *Kiplinger's Personal Finance* (monthly), and *Smart Money* (monthly).

- Most of the news magazines also have on-line services. You can access these sites by using the newspaper or magazine name. For example, www.kiplinger.com gives all sorts of information on investment choices and lets you do calculations on your holdings. The site at www.smartmoney.com offers a free tutorial called Investing 101. The site also lets you enter your own investments, or pretend investments, and then gives you daily updates on your holdings.

Are there any resources for investment information especially for young investors?

- The most exciting way to learn about money, saving, and investing is on-line. There are dozens of interactive sites where you can play investing games and even set up a virtual portfolio. Many of these sites provide current stock prices when you fill in a stock symbol.

- A major resource for young investors is the Homework Center, which is put together by the Multnomah County Library (www.multnomah.lib.or.us/lib/homework/perfinhc.html.) I have this site on my home page as one of my favorites, and I happily wander around in it learning all sorts of things. I'm going to point out some key sources from it below, but you should check out the full site yourself. There's even a place where you can play the stock market by investing in movie stocks.

- One of the best resources on the Homework Center site is www.virtualstockexchange.com. You can learn the basics on everything you need to know about the market. All you have to do is click on a topic in the Investment Guide and head off to the land of stocks or bonds or stock exchanges. There are lists of books as well as information on investment strategies and financial planning. You can set up your own virtual portfolio and practice making trades. You can even enter competitions with other young investors. It's a great site.

- For investor training and market data go to www.investor.nasd.com. One of the most fun parts of this site is a kid's calculator. When you fill in an amount to save, it tells you how much you will have in 10 years, in 25 years, and at age 65. You can even click on the cost of a fast food meal or a pair of running shoes and it will tell you how much you could have saved if you didn't eat out that day or buy those shoes.

- There is a NOVA presentation that tells the history of money and how U.S. money is printed and minted at www.pbs.org/wgbh/nova/moolah/. It teaches you a lot, plus it's illustrated with time lines and pictures of money.

- A U.S. Treasury site that tells you everything you need to know about U.S. Savings Bonds—where to buy them, interest rates, and how to redeem them—is at www.treas.gov/opc/.

- The Dow is found on-line at www.dowjones.com. You can go in a lot of directions from this site, all of which are fun.

- NASDAQ's on-line site is at www.nasdaq.com. You can view the NASDAQ tower and the MarketSite Studio, plus get information on visits.

- You can find free business news from Reuters—one of the major news sources in the world—at www.moneynet.com.

Are there any banks that let kids have checking accounts?
I only know of one bank that is specifically for young investors. It's called the Young Americans Bank. Unlike other banks, the Young Americans Bank will open checking accounts for anyone age 12 and older. Young investors can even open a business checking account. If you are under 18 you have to have an adult co-sign the checks. An ATM card comes with your account, too. The Young Americans Bank will open a savings account with as little as $10. You can also buy certificates of deposit. Finally, they send step-by-step directions for filling out a signature card. A signature card prevents anyone else from forging your name.

It doesn't matter what state you live in; you can mail in your checks or make withdrawals by mail. Here's the address:

Young Americans Bank
311 Steele Street
Denver, Colorado 80206
(303) 321-BANK

Do I need more than money to open a savings or checking account?

Yes. You need a Social Security number (SSN). Everyone in the United States needs a Social Security number. In fact, in most states, just being born gives you a Social Security number. It used to be that Social Security numbers were needed only if you worked. Now, your Social Security number is used for a lot of things such as health insurance and opening bank accounts.

What are the names of some mutual fund families that let you open an account with as little as $1,000 and do not charge a commission?

- Dreyfus Founders (800) 334-6899 or www.dreyfus.com

- Evergreen (800) 343-2898 or www.evergreen.com

- Oakmark (800) 625-6275 or www.oakmark.com

- Schwab (800) 266-5623 or www.schwab.com

There are other large mutual fund families that do not charge a commission, like American Century, Janus, and Vanguard, but these funds require beginning investment amounts of at least $2,500.

What are the names of some on-line brokers?

- Ameritrade (800) 454-9272 or www.ameritrade.com

- Datek On-line (888) 463-2835 or www.datek.com

- E*Trade (800) 786-2575 or www.etrade.com

- Fidelity (800) 544-7272 or www.fidelity.com

- Morgan Stanley Dean Witter (800) 584-6837 or www.on-line.msdw.com

- National Discount Brokers (800) 888-3999 or www.nbd.com

- My Discount Broker (888) 882-5600 or www.mydiscountbroker.com

- Quick & Reilly (800) 837-7220 or www.qron-line.com

- Charles Schwab (800) 435-4000 or www.schwab.com

Some of the on-line brokers offer special services like market information and on-line lessons on investing basics. Fees for trades vary according to the extra services offered, so always check the price. Since you can get on-line training from a number of the sites I've listed above, you don't need to pay for anything but the actual trade costs.

What does it mean when people talk about a bull or a bear market?

Bulls and bears are used as symbols for the stock market—a raging bull and a sleeping bear. A *bull market* is one in which investors have confidence in the economy and buy stocks. The stock market goes up over a period of months or years. A *bear market* is one where the market is sluggish and investors are selling stocks and waiting to see what happens. The stock market goes down over a period of months or years. You will also hear investors referred to as "bullish" or "bearish" about the stock market. This means the same thing as above but it refers to how individuals choose to invest.

Do I have to pay taxes on the money I earn on my savings account and investments?

Yes, if you are 14 or older. If you are under 14, you are allowed to earn $1,400 a year on your investments without paying taxes to the U.S. government. If your savings and investment accounts earn more than $1,400 a year, the excess will be taxed at your parents' income tax rate. This is because the U.S. government wants to get its share of your investment earnings, and it assumes your parents are controlling your money. If you are over 14, you are taxed on your investment earnings at your own income tax rate. The rate is based on the amount of money you have earned.

Is there an on-line source that calculates compound interest?
Yes, here's one: www.bankrate.com/brm/calc/math_smm.asp.

What are some of the categories for mutual funds that I'll see most often?

- **Balanced**: A fund that is a combination of common and preferred stocks. There's a low risk of loss on the original investment and a pretty good chance for long-term growth. These are classified as Growth and Income Fund.

- **Equity income**: Blue-chip stocks and utilities that pay high dividends. These funds involve limited risk to your original investment with medium long-term growth. These are classified as a Growth and Income Fund.

- **Aggressive growth**: Stocks of new companies or companies that fund managers think are selling for less than they are worth. These involve above-average risk. These are classified as a Growth Fund.

- **Emerging markets**: Stocks in companies in developing countries like Mexico or Russia that involve more risk than other growth fund types. These are classified as a Growth Fund.

- **Small-cap**: Stocks in new companies that have a limited amount of capital behind them. These have a higher level of risk. They're classified as a Growth Fund.

- **Mid-cap**: Stocks in companies that have a moderate level of capital, have a medium level of risk, and are classified as a Growth Fund.

- **Large-cap**: Stocks in well-established companies that have a large amount of capital, a lower level of risk, and are classified as a Growth and Income Fund.

Are there any books that I should know about?

- *The Wall Street Journal Guide to Understanding Money & Investing,* by Kenneth M. Morris and Virginia B. Morris. (New York: Lightbulb Press, Inc., 1999). This is a clear and easy-to-use guide to money, stocks, bonds, mutual funds, and the stock market. It also covers the Federal Reserve Board and the economy. Plus, it's small and easy to carry in a backpack. It's written for adults, but clear enough for investors of all ages.

- *The Wall Street Journal Interactive Editions Guide to On-line Investing,* by Dave Pettit and Rich Jaroslovsky. (New York: Crown Publishers, 2000). A recent publication, this book tells you everything you need to know about on-line investing. It includes a lot of contact names, phone numbers, and on-line addresses. It's written for adults, but it can be used as a resource by all ages.

- *The 100 Best Stocks You Can Buy,* by John Slatter. (Holbrook, MA: Adams Media Corporation, 2000). This is an excellent resource for collecting information on stocks. Although the author includes only 100 stock companies, each company is considered a good buy for an individual investor. Each of the stocks I've used as examples are discussed in Slatter's book. This book is written for adults, but it can be used as a resource by all ages.

- *10-Minute Guide to the Stock Market,* by Dian Vujovich. (New York: Alpha Books, 1997). This is a guide to stocks and the stock market divided into 18 short chapters. It's clear and easy to read. It's written for adults, but readable for all ages.

How do I order the video titled *The Great Game*, which explains all about Wall Street?

Send a $25 check with your mailing address to: Burrelle's Transcripts, P.O. Box 7, Livingston, NJ, 07039, or call (800) 777-8398. If you call to order a copy over the phone, a credit card is required, and you'll be assessed an additional $3 processing fee.

Are there other things to invest in beside stocks, bonds, and mutual funds?

Yes, there are a lot of other things, such as real estate. Remember, Billy Ray invested in land. People also invest in collectibles. *Collectibles* are things that have a value that may increase above what you paid for them, such as baseball cards, old records, or first-edition books that still have their original book jackets. Some people collect Civil War items, arrowheads, or signed baseballs; other people collect coins, including old coins, newly minted coins, and special edition coins. My youngest grandson collects key chains. They may be worth a lot in the future, especially if the time comes that all doors are opened electronically and we don't have to use keys anymore. A lot of people also buy art with the hope that the artist will become famous and the art will increase in value. Almost anything you can think of can be collected, and if you choose your collections well, you can enjoy them now and eventually sell them for a profit.

Thinking of More Questions

Ask some investment questions of your own. Are there any other questions that you want answered? Figure out where to go for the information you need. Drop me a card with your question. If I update this book, then I'll be able to include these questions with answers.

Conclusion

THE WRAP-UP, INCLUDING A
REMINDER OF THE GOAL

THAT'S IT. WE'RE done. If you've gotten to this point and read every word—or nearly every word—you know a lot about investing, more than most people, adults included! All your knowledge adds up to one thing: you are now fluent in the language of business—you know the words to use and how to use them. That makes me very proud, and you should be proud, too.

What happened to Billy Ray since he decided to build equity in his farm? By Thanksgiving 2000, Billy Ray was 23. He graduated from Georgetown College with a double major in business and communications. He was no longer playing basketball, but he's still known as "the Legend." In fact, in March 2001, Billy Ray's name was added to the

Tenth Region Basketball Hall of Fame. He decided he wanted to get a real estate license so he could help other people buy and sell houses, so he studied hard and passed the Kentucky real estate exam. Now he has his license, but that's not his main job.

Billy Ray thought a lot about what he wanted to do after college, and he shopped around for jobs. He decided to take a job with a bank working as a loan officer. A *loan officer* looks at the assets and equity of people who want to take out loans from the bank, and then he decides if the bank should lend money to people—just as Billy Ray did when he wanted small business or home mortgage loans. Now Billy Ray's the one making the lending decisions.

On February 24, 2001, Billy Ray married his college sweetheart, Micah Robinson. The garage is finished and they have turned it into a house.

As you can imagine, Billy Ray hasn't stopped planning. He thinks that the next thing he wants to do is to buy a piece of investment property, like a house or apartment building that he can rent out. He wants to find something where the rents will pay the cost of the mortgage loan. With a little invested in upkeep, he'll be able to sit back and wait for the value of the property to go up. Knowing Billy Ray, he'll probably figure out a way to make this happen. He probably won't stop there, either. All the time he's making these investment plans, his three mutual funds are working away for him. Sometimes they're all earning money for him and sometimes one may lose a little, but over time his investments are building assets—just as Billy Ray planned.

GLOSSARY

AMEX: American Stock Exchange, also called "the Curb."

APR: Annual or annualized percentage rate.

Assets: The value of an individual's or company's property and possessions.

ATM: Automated Teller Machine. Machines placed in convenient locations that allow you to withdraw money from or deposit money into your checking or savings accounts.

Back-end load: The commission paid to the broker or fund family when selling shares in a mutual fund. The fees are stated in percentages of the total dollar amount of the trade.

Bank statement: A monthly record from the bank that lists the checks that have been paid from and the deposits made to an account. The end number is the balance of your account on the date the bank mailed the statement.

Bond: An agreement between two parties allowing one to borrow money from the other for a set period of time in return for interest.

Broker: A person who buys or sells stocks or bonds for individual investors through an exchange. All brokers have to pass a national test in order to trade stocks and bonds.

Brokerage house: An investment company that is a member of a stock exchange. The membership allows the brokerage house to trade stocks through the exchange.

Capital: The money or other assets that a company uses to start and then operate a business.

Certificate of Deposit (CD): A savings device that pays interest based on a deposit for a specified length of time. The longer the term of the certificate agreement, the higher the interest rate paid.

Check register: The section in a checkbook where each check written is entered.

Checking account: Money deposited in a bank and used to make purchases in place of cash. The money in the account is accessed by writing checks that are provided in a checkbook or by doing ATM transactions.

Compound interest: One method of accumulating interest over time. Interest is added to the original savings amount at set time periods, such as once a month, and the saver earns interest on the interest paid the previous month. Compounding periods can vary from daily to monthly to quarterly (3 months) to semiannually (6 months).

Consumer confidence: Consumers' (or "spenders'") attitudes about the health of the economy. Confidence determines how freely consumers will spend.

Corporate bond: A contract between an investor and a private company. The investor agrees to lend the company money for a set period of time and, in exchange, the investor receives interest paid by the company.

Credit card: A card that allows you to make a purchase without cash, with the understanding that you will pay at a later date.

Debit card: A card that allows you to purchase items with money from your checking account without writing a check.

Dividend Reinvestment Plan (DRIP): An agreement between an investor and a company that allows the investor to buy more stock with his dividends, instead of taking the dividends in cash.

Dow Jones Industrial Average (DJIA), or "the Dow": The daily closing price—shown as an average—of 30 stocks listed on the New York Stock Exchange. The Dow is used as a scorecard for the stock market for the day.

Economics: The science of the production and distribution of wealth.

Economist: A person who studies and manages the production and distribution of wealth.

Economy: The wealth and resources of communities of all sizes, such as towns, cities, states, and nations. The word economy comes from a Greek word that means household management.

Equity: The remaining value of a piece of property, after subtracting the amount left to pay on the mortgage. You must take into account both the amount of the loan already paid back and the increased or decreased value of the property to get an accurate equity amount.

Federal Reserve System, or "the Fed": The United States' national banking system.

Front-end load: The commission paid to the broker or fund family when purchasing shares in a mutual fund. The fees are stated in percentages of the dollar amount of the trade.

Inflation: An increase in prices. When prices go up, the value of money goes down because it cannot buy as much.

Interest: Money paid for the use of money lent.

Invest: To commit money in order to earn a financial return.

Limit order: A stock sale or purchase made at a price that is above or below the set price order. A limit order will only be filled if it is to the investor's benefit. The order can be open for a day ("day order") or until the investor cancels it ("good 'til cancelled order," or "GTC").

Line of credit: A set amount of money available to borrow against as needed. Interest is charged only on the amount of money borrowed, not on the total amount of credit available.

Macroeconomics: The branch of economics that studies the big picture, such as how many people are working, what they are getting paid, and how many trucks and cars are being produced.

Market order: A stock trade made at the current market price. The stock shares are bought or sold as soon as the broker places the order.

Microeconomics: The branch of economics that studies individual companies and the consumer response to them.

Money market account: A type of savings account purchased through a bank or investment company. Money market accounts offer higher interest rates than straight savings accounts.

Mortgage: A contract between a borrower and lender to buy property. The lender is usually a bank or savings and loan company. The borrower pays the lender interest on a monthly basis for the use of the money.

Municipal bond: A contract between an investor and a municipality. The investor agrees to lend the municipality money for a set period of time, and in exchange the investor receives interest paid by the municipality.

Mutual fund: An investment company that buys groups of stocks or bonds to fit a certain investment goal. Investors are sold shares in the fund.

NASDAQ: National Association of Securities Dealers Automated Quotation.

NYSE: New York Stock Exchange.

Portfolio: The stocks and bonds in a mutual fund. Portfolio also means the stocks and bonds owned by an investor.

Portfolio manager: A person trained to buy and sell stocks or bonds in order to meet the goals of a stock or bond fund.

Principal: The original sum of an investment.

Recession: A temporary decline in prosperity and economic activity.

Return: The profit of an investment.

Risk tolerance: The level of risk that a person feels comfortable taking.

Savings account: Money kept by a bank or savings and loan company. The bank or savings and loan company pays you interest to use your money for its lending business.

Savings and loan companies: Privately owned companies that offer savings accounts at slightly higher rates of interest than banks. Savings and loan companies also lend money.

Securities and Exchange Commission (SEC) or "the Commission": The controlling body in charge of stock and bond markets in the United States. The SEC sets the rules for the stock and bond markets, investigates problems, and sets penalties.

Shareholder: A person who owns a share of stock in a company.

Simple interest: A percentage of interest paid for a set period of time, such as six months or one year.

Stock: The capital of a company.

Stock exchange: Company where shares of stock are bought and sold.

Stock share: A portion of the capital of a company.

Stop order: A stock trade at a set price. The stock shares are bought or sold the moment the market price hits the price set by the investor. The order can be open for a day ("day order") or until the investor cancels it ("good 'til cancelled order," or "GTC").

Treasury bill, note, and bond: A contract between an investor and the U.S. government. The investor agrees to lend the government money for a set period of time, and in exchange the investor receives interest paid by the government.

United States Savings Bond: A specific type of contract between an investor and the U.S. government. The government agrees to pay the individual an agreed upon amount of money in exchange for a loan for a set number of years.

Yield: The profit on an investment.

Index

AUTHOR BIOGRAPHY

Katherine R. Bateman was born in Ashland, Kentucky, in 1940, and she has had diverse interests for as long as she can remember. In her first career she was an art historian and college professor. She received her B.A. from Berea College in Berea, Kentucky, and her M.A. and Ph.D. from the University of Michigan in Ann Arbor, with postdoctoral work at the University of Chicago. She taught art history at Berea College and the School of the Art Institute of Chicago. During this career she published articles and presented research papers on early medieval manuscripts and ivories, and she developed courses on women in art. After 13 years of teaching and administration, she decided to start over.

Her second career was in business. In 1983 she joined Nuveen Investments to assist the director of the firm's research and managed funds group, and she began to teach herself the language of business. During this career she published handbooks to guide brokers and their clients on various topics, including savings programs for college educations and retirement, and she served as manager of the higher education sector in Nuveen's research group.

She was also active in the National Federation of Municipal Analysts (NFMA), which represents institutional investors. In her capacity with the NFMA she worked closely with the Securities and Exchange Commission to develop industry guidelines for the municipal market and testified before Congress regarding regulation of municipal bonds. She was named the leading analyst in higher education by the *Bond Buyer*, *Institutional Investor*, and *Smith's Research and Ratings Review*, and won awards for her work on ongoing disclosure with NFMA.

In the spring of 2000, Bateman retired from Nuveen Investments to write books—a desire she has had since childhood. She continues to serve as the financial advisor for the Illinois Educational Facilities Authority, a position she has held for the past six years.